ROMANCING THE CUSTOMER

Maximizing Brand Value Through
Powerful Relationship Management

ROMANCING THE CUSTOMER

Maximizing Brand Value Through
Powerful Relationship Management

Paul Temporal
and
Martin Trott

John Wiley & Sons (Asia) Pte Ltd

Singapore   New York   Chichester
Brisbane   Toronto   Weinheim

Copyright © 2001 John Wiley & Sons (Asia) Pte Ltd
Published by John Wiley & Sons (Asia) Pte Ltd
2 Clementi Loop, #02-01, Singapore 129809

This publication is designed to provide accurate and authoritative information in
regard to the subject matter covered. It is sold with the understanding that the Publisher
is not engaged in rendering professional services. If professional advice or other expert
assistance is required, the services of a competent professional person should be sought.

Other Wiley Editorial Offices

John Wiley & Sons, Inc., 605 Third Avenue, New York, NY 10158-0012, USA
John Wiley & Sons Ltd, Baffins Lane, Chichester, West Sussex PO19 1UD, England
John Wiley & Sons (Canada) Ltd, 22 Worcester Road, Rexdale, Ontario M9W 1L1, Canada
John Wiley & Sons Australia Ltd, 33 Park Road (PO Box 1226), Milton, Queensland 4046,
Australia
Wiley-VCH, Pappelallee 3, 69469 Weinheim, Germany

Library of Congress Cataloging-in-Publication Data:

Temporal, Paul.
    Romancing the Customer: maximizing brand value through powerful relationship
    management/
Paul Temporal and Martin Trott.
        p. cm.
    Includes index.
    ISBN 0-471-84615-5
        1. Relationship marketing. 2. Brand name products—Marketing. I. Trott, Martin. II.
Title.

HF5415.55.T46 2001
658.8'27—dc21   2001020262

Typeset in 11/15 point, Goudy by Linographic Services Pte Ltd
Printed in Singapore by Saik Wah Press Pte Ltd
10 9 8 7 6 5 4 3 2 1

To our families

Contents

Acknowledgments

In the writing of any business book, there are always many people and companies that are not only co-operative, but really helpful, and we would like to thank everyone for their assistance, particularly the following organizations:

AKuP International Inc
Brand Finance plc
Edaran Otomobil Nasional
its4me plc
Malaysia Airlines
Oracle Corporation
Pan Pacific Hotels and Resorts
Relationship Marketing International
RMI Network Sdn. Bhd.
SAP
Sony (India)
Sony (Australia)

In addition, we would like to say special thanks to the following individuals:

Alex Hu
B.S. Retnam
Ch'ng Teik Cheng
Chris Davies
David Haigh
Fauziah Abdul Aziz
Hong Seok Lin
Ichigo Umehara
Jade Ong
Khatijah Shah Mohamed
Patrick Smith
Paul Cheall
Raj Kumar
Ravi Parasuram
Steve Halliday

Thanks also to Nick Wallwork and Janis Soo of John Wiley & Sons (Asia) for their usual splendid CRM performance, and Robyn Flemming for editing the manuscript.

We owe all of you a lot – thanks.

Preface

A revolution is taking place in the world of branding. Essentially, agencies, companies, and individuals involved in the branding process appear to be shifting their focus from the visual aspects of identity and design to the realms of brand strategy and the customer experience. In other words, brand management is now gearing up toward not just making promises but actually delivering on them. The focus has now moved from the creative to the customer. And not before time!

Customer relationship management (CRM) has been particularly influential in triggering this shift of thought and action. Before its renaissance over the last few years, only the powerful brands of the world, and those companies with a clear understanding of what a brand strategy is all about, had really bothered about the brand experience and realized how powerful it could be in building both sustainable competitive advantage and profitability.

The advent of CRM techniques—not new in concept, but new in their form of execution—has lifted the veil of helplessness from many marketers' eyes, by showing them how, at last, marketing in a true one-to-one sense can actually be achieved. And not through loyalty schemes and the like, but through real one-to-one relationships, where each customer is treated differently.

Others have written about CRM and one-to-one marketing, but what they have failed to do is link CRM with the brand-building process. It is in the realm of building brand equity and value, and in speeding up that process, that CRM makes its real contribution. This book is about this link and more. It not only shows how CRM can drive brand power and value, but also describes how CRM works and how all companies can implement its principles in a very practical way.

ROMANCING THE CUSTOMER

Sadly, for many companies in the last century, building powerful brands often took decades. This fact alone dissuaded many CEOs from even starting to take brand building seriously. Then along came CRM in the late 1990s, aimed at enabling companies to do all these things in a new way, and *voilà*! everything changed. Now brands can be built in just a few years. The world of branding has now embraced CRM, and the strategic role of CRM is to build brands. When done well, CRM programs help to build brands by contributing to all eight of the key characteristics of brands (described in Chapter 1). And as far as the brand–customer relationship is concerned, the end result is "*Je t'aime*."

We have called this book *Romancing the Customer* because the ideas it contains will help you to make your customers feel happy, appreciated, and even loved. The book will map out how you can build your company's brand name by achieving a special relationship with each and every customer. By so doing, it will help you to:

- achieve greater levels of customer acquisition and retention;
- become outstanding at service quality;
- build your profit margins through bigger price premiums;
- achieve a sustainable competitive advantage;
- increase the asset value of your company; and
- give each of your customers that warm glow that comes with feeling appreciated and cared for.

As you will see, the ways in which you can employ the techniques of CRM will transform the development and management of your brand. But the book won't only show you how massive the impact can be; you will also be shown many ways of improving your business, just one or two of which can change your company's future and success. If you take all of them on board, your brand will soar far and away above those of your competitors. And so will its financial value.

THE READER

In looking at the readership for this book, we feel that it will be of real benefit to:

- CEOs, CFOs, and CTOs;
- marketing directors and managers;

- brand and category managers;
- customer managers (few though they may be);
- entrepreneurs;
- marketing, brand, and management consultants;
- customer service managers;
- students of business and management;

and all those who want to survive in an increasingly competitive world, where only the strong brands will survive.

1

CRM and Brand Value

THE DRIVE TOWARD LEVERAGING THE CORPORATE BRAND

There has been a marked change in direction by companies around the world, away from concentrating on product branding and toward focusing on the corporate brand. Even the masters of product branding, Procter & Gamble, are now putting significantly more strategic effort into leveraging the corporate brand name. There are many reasons for this. When a company is creating and building brands independently, with little endorsement from the parent, it is an expensive exercise. Product branding requires each brand to stand on its own and have its own investment, which in research and development (R&D) and advertising and promotion (A&P) alone can be enormous. With little parental support, getting through the stages of brand awareness and acceptance in the marketplace can be highly resource consuming, which is one of the reasons why Unilever is reducing the number of its brands from 1,600 to 400. With corporate branding, most frequently seen where the company adds its name to the product brands it launches, there is the added value of trust and the shared synergies of the other investments needed. But one of the main determinants of this trend is the fact that brands can be valued in financial terms.

It is now widely acknowledged that brands, if created, developed, and managed well, can achieve spectacular financial results. If we look at the market capitalization of heavily branded companies versus unbranded companies in both the U.S. and the U.K., the S&P and FTSE markets

1

respectively, we see that around 70% or more of the market capitalization is not represented by the net asset value of the companies concerned. In some industries, such as telecommunications, this figure is over 90%! There is a huge gap between market capitalization and net tangible assets, and intangible assets represent this unexplained value, a significant part being the value of the brand itself. Other intangible items include patents, customer lists, licenses, know how, and major contracts, but the value of the brand itself is increasingly becoming the biggest item. Brand names are often worth multiples of the value of the actual business. As a result, brands are often bought and sold for considerable amounts of money, which represent not so much the tangible assets belonging to the company, but the expectation of the brand's level of sales into the foreseeable future.

A strong corporate brand name brings with it additional financial strength which can be measured and used in many ways, including:

♦ **Mergers and acquisitions**: Brand valuation plays a major part in these undertakings. Potential acquirers of branded goods companies, together with their investors and bankers, want to know that the company's price can be substantiated by reference to the value of the specific assets being acquired.

♦ **External investor relations**: For some major companies, building a portfolio of world-class brands is a central objective. Brand valuation can be used to provide hard numbers in what is often a soft argument.

♦ **Internal communications**: Brand valuation can help explain performance and be used as a means of motivating management. The use of internal royalty rates based on brand values can also make clear to a group of companies the value of the corporate assets they are being allowed to use.

♦ **Marketing budget allocation**: Brand valuation can assist in budgeting decisions, providing a more systematic basis for decision making.

♦ **Internal marketing management**: Strategic use of brand valuation techniques allows senior management to compare the success of different brand strategies and the relative performance of particular marketing teams.

- ◆ **Balance sheet reporting**: In certain parts of the world, acquired brands are now carried as intangible assets and amortized.

- ◆ **Licensing and franchising**: Accurate brand valuation allows a realistic set of charges to be created for the licensing and franchising of brand names.

- ◆ **Securitized borrowing**: Companies such as Disney and Levi Strauss have borrowed major sums against their brand names.

- ◆ **Litigation support**: Brand valuations have been used in legal cases to defend the brand value, such as in illicit use of a brand name or receivership.

- ◆ **Fair trading investigations**: Brand valuation has been used to explain to non-marketing audiences the role of brands, and the importance their value has for the companies that spend so much to acquire and maintain them.

- ◆ **Tax planning**: More and more companies are actively planning the most effective domicile for their brand portfolios with branded royalty streams in mind.

- ◆ **New product and market development assessment**: New business strategies can be modeled using brand valuation techniques to make judgments on, for example, best brand, best market extension, and best consumer segment.

THE DIFFERENCE BETWEEN BRAND VALUE AND BRAND EQUITY

There is a distinct difference between brand value and brand equity, but unfortunately the two are often confused. When we talk about *brand value*, we mean the actual financial worth of the brand. *Brand equity*, on the other hand, is often used in referring to the descriptive aspects of a brand, whether symbols, imagery, or consumer associations. It is a term used to represent the more subjective and intangible views of the brand as held by consumers, and is somewhat misleading, as the word "equity" has a financial origin.

American professor David Aaker describes brand equity, as opposed to brand value, and has developed what he calls the Brand Equity Ten—

the 10 key aspects of brand performance or strength, as he sees it. They are:

- *Price premium*—the additional price that consumers will pay for the brand.
- *Satisfaction/loyalty*—levels of satisfaction with the brand that help determine loyalty and price sensitivity.
- *Perceived quality*—relative to other brands.
- *Leadership/popularity*—in terms of market leadership.
- *Perceived value*—a value-for-money concept linked to quality.
- *Brand personality*—the characteristics of the brand's "persona" that differentiate it from others.
- *Organizational associations*—including trust.
- *Brand awareness*—a key measure of brand strength.
- *Market share*—a link between volume and perceived value.
- *Market price and distribution coverage*—including distribution percentage.

Whilst recommending these as almost a scorecard for use, Aaker admits there is no absolute score for these dimensions, but suggests that this mix of attitudinal, behavioral, and market measures of brand equity should be the focus for good brand management practice. What is interesting with his classification is that it contains a mixture of what we would see as some of the drivers of both brand value and brand equity. Calculating brand value is, of course, a very specialized area, and the key drivers of brand performance are not all contained in the above list, but there is a substantial overlap. For those readers interested in establishing the financial value of brands, Brand Finance plc is a company that is expert in this area. A visit to their website, www.brandfinance.com, is a good starting point.

Thus, although there is a difference in terminology, it appears that there is a connection between brand value and brand equity, because many of the components of brand equity have been found to be the drivers of brand value. While we don't need to go into detail here about the methodologies involved in calculating brand equity and brand value, the point we want to make is that companies wishing to achieve spectacular rates of return on investment should be concentrating on building up the strength of the corporate brand name in their chosen markets. Whichever list or source you look at with regard to the components of brand equity and value, it quickly becomes apparent that the only route to doing this is to concentrate on providing consumers with the best possible brand experience, and this is where CRM contributes heavily.

BRAND VALUE, EQUITY, AND CRM

CRM represents a fantastic opportunity for anyone wishing to build a corporate brand, because it helps in the rapid buildup of both brand equity and brand value. Certainly, with its individual attention and customization, it impacts highly on issues such as perceived quality, satisfaction and loyalty, perceived personality, leadership and popularity. When successful, the rapid spread of its notoriety and achievement build up the opportunities for price premiums. Additionally, it creates differentiation and helps to grow market share, and by so doing builds the financial value of the brand. These are compelling arguments for any company considering the introduction of a CRM program.

However, there is one more monumental argument in favor of CRM: it helps to build brands *quickly*. It accelerates both the learning curve about the customer and the development of the brand–customer relationship. It is the future of brand building. It is relevant now to explain why CRM fits so well with the nature of brands and how they are built.

KEY CHARACTERISTICS OF BRANDS— THE CRM FIT

Let's look at some of the key facts about brand building, and how well CRM fits into these.

1. **Brands are relationships**: People don't buy *products*; they buy *brands*, for the reasons described below.

2. **Brands are experiences**: As with every relationship, it is the experience that makes the difference. A *good* experience with anything or anyone fuels the desire for more, while a poor experience kills the appetite. Similarly, a *consistently* good experience leads to familiarity, friendship, and intimacy, while inconsistent experiences lead to doubts and distancing. Power brands generate consistently good experiences, whether they originate from companies, products, or services.

3. **Brands are very personal**: People make friends with brands because they give them the opportunity for a relationship and good experiences. It is the very nature of the relationship and experience as interpreted by each consumer that makes the brand special and personal to each. Brands give exclusivity of feeling and association. Look at the way in which some people lovingly wash their car or touch their clothing. The brand is very special to them.

4. **Brands evoke emotion**: Perhaps one of the most amazing facts about brands is that they can evoke emotion in people. Sometimes, this emotion is so strong it can influence people's behavior. For instance, in Tokyo, people have been mugged specifically for their Nike trainers! Many people are intrigued by how powerful brand-related emotions can be, and mystified as to how brands are built with this in mind. Emotion is often at the very heart of power brand strategies, aiming to capture both the rational and emotional aspects of the target consumers.

5. **Brands live and evolve**: Brands are very much like people. Many of the world's strongest brands have their own distinctive personalities, just as we do, and these personalities evolve over time, just as ours do. They have their own values and beliefs that guide their basic behavior. They act consistently, and yet adapt to new surroundings and situations, showing the ability to grow, learn, and develop. They have longevity, where products do not, and can continue to be relevant to changing times.

6. **Brands communicate:** Like people, brands listen, receive feedback, and send messages. They even talk to different people in different ways, just as we do. Brands that are successful tend to be those that achieve a dialogue with consumers, and, as in our human world, those that can communicate well are respected and valued by society.

7. **Brands create equity and loyalty:** It is the strength of brand associations, feelings, and emotions that tends to provide brands with the equity they acquire. It is the way in which brands interact, and the friendship they give, that engenders loyalty and a long-lasting relationship. It is a combination of all the above strengths that also adds financial value to the brand.

8. **Brands, above all, add friendship and romance:** It is true to say that brands, as shown by the above, really do become friends with the people who buy them. The greater the emotional involvement on the part of the consumer, the greater the friendship and loyalty that results. Some people have a lifelong love for their brands, an unsatisfied desire always to be with them and near them, to talk about them and relate to them. Brands can add romance to the lives of the most ordinary of people.

The eight points set out above make a formidable and powerful list of branding benefits. Getting brands to achieve these results is not easy, but CRM can help to accelerate the process. The world's most powerful brands are those that consistently delight consumers, and CRM—as a package of knowledge and techniques—is aimed precisely at establishing customer delight.

2

CRM Explained

WHAT IS CRM?

This chapter explains briefly what CRM is and how everyone in the organization has a role to play in a CRM program. How CRM is positioned prior to a program being introduced is critical to its success, and we will address this issue also in this chapter. But let's look first at what "CRM" means.

Customer relationship management is sometimes called customer relationship marketing, or just relationship marketing. We prefer not to use the term "relationship marketing," as it is often used to mean points programs such as frequent flyer programs, which to us do not constitute real CRM.

CRM is all about collaborating with each customer—being able to create the classic win–win situation: you add value to each customer's daily life, and they give you loyalty in return. It is, in fact, about dealing with each customer individually. Frequent flyer programs and other points-based loyalty schemes do not really do this.

Traditionally, marketing textbooks have suggested that "all customers are equal." But does that old adage really make sense? We all know about, and subscribe to, the Pareto principle (the 80:20 rule). So, if 20% of your customers represent 80% of your revenue, or 10% of your customers represent 90% of your profits, it is clear that all customers are *not* equal. CRM recognizes this—different customers represent a different value to your organization. But CRM takes it one step further by suggesting that if this is the case, *they should not be treated equally.*

The purpose of CRM programs, then, is to recognize the best customers (we will explain later what this means) and hold on to them by increasing your understanding of their needs as individuals, meeting the expectations they have of your organization, and making a difference to their lives.

Managing profitable and unprofitable customers

CRM is also about looking at customers who may not be big spenders now, but who *could* be if they are encouraged by a really good brand experience. While the economics of focusing on your most profitable customers are compelling, a good CRM program should not ignore all the others. Sure, the level of attention less profitable customers may get (and deserve) may be somewhat lower, but the principles can apply at all levels. In fact, CRM programs encourage customers who are not very profitable to move up into more profitable segments.

If you are starting from a position of little or no knowledge about your customer base, the task you need to undertake is not unlike that of a fisherman. You need to cast your net wide, in order to pull as many customers into the net of your program as possible. Once you have them on board, you can take a good look at them and decide which ones to hold on to and which ones to throw back. You might also want to tag a few of the "middlers" who are showing growth potential, so that you can track them and bring them on to be like the big fish. So, your task is to find out how to bring them into the net to begin with, and then to decide which ones to keep, which ones to throw back, and which ones to keep a watchful eye on.

There is no doubt that by turning your organization into one that is centered around the customer, every single customer will ultimately benefit in one way or another. Because once you begin to alter the culture of an organization and your people get used to thinking "customer first," it is virtually impossible to go back to the old way. So, even though a particular customer ultimately may not be among the elite ranks of your "Premier Customer" group, or may not hold your "Titanium" card, they will enjoy the benefits of all the positive changes that have percolated their way through your company.

CRM is about capturing "share of heart," not "share of wallet"

Some people talk about the aim of CRM as being to capture "share of wallet"—in other words, trying to increase the portion of each customer's spend that comes to you. You might build up short-term sales by this type of money-grabbing thinking, but you cannot build an enduring relationship. We prefer to think of it as capturing "share of heart"—that is, creating an emotional bond with your customers such that they pledge allegiance to your brand. If you achieve this allegiance, "share of wallet" will be a natural by-product. In the long term, if you appeal to the hearts of these customers, they will themselves become part of your best salesforce—by being your happy, and thus loyal, customers and advocates.

THE RISE OF CRM

Let's have a look at why CRM is being embraced so rapidly around the world, by starting with an interesting quotation.

Business is entering a new era, "the information economy," the distinguishing characteristic of which is a change in the fundamental drivers of wealth creation from tangible assets of land, labor and wealth to intangibles—the development and exploitation of ideas, knowledge and information. In doing so it is transforming marketing. Marketing theory and practice developed for the industrial economy does not necessarily fit the new emerging economy. (*Financial Times Report: Brand Strategies in the Information Age. The Rise of New Marketing*, January 1998)

The way in which we market our products and services to customers has undergone rapid change in the last decade or so. Unfortunately, the marketing textbooks have been slow to catch up: for the most part, they continue to advocate the same old techniques that have been practiced for many years.

But times have changed, and these old techniques are becoming less relevant and increasingly outdated. For instance, many organizations still persist with structures and processes that are geared around product divisions. However, as they awaken to the realization that perhaps the needs of the customer ought to be driving their business, rather than their internal desire to create a nice product, then they will have no choice but to embrace CRM and this new information-led approach.

Many of the traditional marketing textbooks have made marketing sound like a numbers game—and in some fields, you could probably construct a reasonable argument to suggest that it still is. But what *makes* marketing a numbers game is a lack of sufficient *information* about people that would enable you to really focus on those people who are likely to be the most responsive to what you place in front of them. This remains the holy grail of the direct marketer.

It has been the phenomenal rise and accessibility of computing power over the last 20 years that has enabled us to move beyond the numbers game, from a blunderbuss approach, to a rifle shot aimed at our primary targets. Most of us now have more computing power on our desktops than most blue chip companies had in their entire organization two decades ago. A typical desktop PC can handle the processing of databases large enough to support most of the marketing campaigns that you or I would be likely to run. So, computing power has increased exponentially, but it has taken us a while to develop our marketing techniques to take full advantage of it.

Tom Peters' groundbreaking book *In Search of Excellence* talked about empowering people to do whatever it took to satisfy the needs and desires of customers. He talked about pushing the decision making down to the shop floor, to the point of interaction with the customer. These were noble ambitions, but ambitions which could only readily be pursued by "new world" companies, companies that didn't have years of history driving rigid management structures, and legacy computer systems which took forever to change. In his follow-up book, *Liberation Management*, Peters acknowledged that these sorts of organizations effectively had to destroy themselves in order to enable the people who worked within them to get closer to the customer.

Some of the biggest companies in the world have long had entirely inwardly focused organizations. Job titles such as "product manager," "brand manager," and "chief marketing officer" indicate the point of focus. But where is the "customer manager" or the "chief relationship officer"? We have seen some companies moving to a "half-way house" of "channel manager"—but what does this really mean? Who is at the end of the "channel"? Is there really such a reluctance to recognize the existence of customers?

Happily, some major organizations, such as Procter & Gamble and Unilever, are taking the lead and creating "customer managers." And if they can do it, so can you. If Unilever, a company with several hundred brands, has recognized that customer managers may be more important to long-term profitability than brand managers, then shouldn't you be giving it some thought? It is not that companies such as these have decided that brand management is now of less importance. On the contrary. They are saying that the best way to build strong brand equity and value is by focusing their efforts on the consumer and not on the product. CRM helps brand management to look from the outside in, rather than from the inside out.

Effective CRM is about using the knowledge you have about your customer, and applying it in such a way that, every time they interact with you, you do something different, better, or more relevant to that person. In other words, you add value to the interaction between you and the customer by reusing information they have previously volunteered to you. By building up that body of knowledge over time, you can increase the degree of tailoring of your product or service and, in the process, strengthen the emotional bond between the customer, your brand, and your company.

BACK TO THE FUTURE?

Contrary to some views, CRM isn't a recently invented technique. In fact, it is often said that there are no new ideas in marketing, and this is certainly true of CRM. Let's look at a simple illustration.

Do you remember the old "Mom and Pop" stores? As long as 40 years or more ago, corner storekeepers were practicing CRM. When we were growing up back in our small villages or suburbs, the neighborhood probably had only one store. The storekeeper, who owned the store, knew everyone in the village or suburb by name. Not only that, but he knew how many people were in each family, the stage of the children's education, and so on. Whenever someone who lived nearby visited the store, the storekeeper would engage in chat with them and take note of the items they bought.

One of our families was typical. Martin's mother would walk to the store at the end of their street, where she would have a long conversation with the storekeeper about her family and the storekeeper's family. The conversation was never about selling products. After they had chatted for a while, Martin's mother would pass her shopping list to the storekeeper and then return home. That afternoon, the shopping would be delivered directly to the family house by the storekeeper, who would carry it into the kitchen. All Martin's mother had to do was put it away in the pantry cupboard.

Many of us have similar memories of being made to feel valued as customers. But with the advent of mass consumption from around the late 1960s, the small stores were displaced by supermarkets, which bought in bulk and gave attractive price discounts, and then by hypermarkets, which did more of the same. However, we had to pay a price for these fabulous deals: we had to drive for miles to get to the supermarket, find a parking place, suffer long queues, and be served by checkout assistants whose attitude showed they cared little about our custom. We gradually realized that we were the ones giving the service, not receiving it.

However, things are beginning to change back again. Look at where the major food retailers are going in the 21st century: you can now send your shopping list to them over the Internet, and they will deliver your order to your home within 24 hours. Forty years on from the Mom and Pop stores, technology is allowing retailers to meet the service standards of the 1960s.

Shopping has become a very impersonal experience, a necessary, oftentimes unpleasant, chore. And the bigger the stores become, the more remote the shopping experience is bound to become. The whole rationale for hypermarkets is to move numbers, big numbers. "Pile 'em high, sell 'em cheap" in its best form. With such a compulsion to move numbers, that is all the customer has become—a number. The supermarket or hypermarket is at the other extreme from the Mom and Pop store. Whereas the supermarket manager is primarily interested in increasing the number of units of beans sold in a day, the Mom and Pop store used other criteria to value its customers. The Mom and Pop store was one of the earliest exponents of marketing based on the lifetime value of a customer, even the lifetime value of generations of a family, because these relationships are potentially so strong they can survive and pass from one generation to another.

THE CONCEPT OF LIFETIME VALUE

Since the 1960s, supermarkets have only been interested in transactional data—how many units of product have been sold today. The same can be said of banks. Only now are they beginning to realize that, through understanding more about the person who is buying the product, they can increase their profit. We will deal with the lifetime value of customers in some detail later. At this stage, all you need to remember is that it is a reflection of how often a customer buys from you, how much they spend when they do buy, when they last bought from you, and what they are likely to buy from you during their lifetime.

A simple example of this is the training that Mercedes-Benz salespeople receive. They are told to imagine that every customer who walks into the showroom has $1 million stuck to their forehead—because that is what they will be worth in sales over their lifetime. Their training teaches them to look beyond the current transaction, which is undoubtedly important to the salesperson wanting to achieve this month's sales target, and to treat the customer in such a way that they will keep coming back to the showroom and buy again and again and again. It is critical to look at customers in terms of their lifetime value, understand what it means to you, and live by it.

IS CRM DIFFERENT FROM ADVERTISING?

To address this question, let's start by separating out the glitzy TV commercials from the rest of the pack. TV commercials—or TVCs, to use the advertising trade jargon—are great for creating general corporate and product awareness, and for brand building. They let the world know that you exist as a company, and what your company does or what it stands for. These are "big broadcast" messages—they are targeted only to the degree that the medium is carefully selected in terms of which channel they are run on and the particular time slot on that channel, but it is very difficult to target specific groups of customers, not to mention individual customers.

Invariably, TVCs are based on monologue; they make a statement, but don't particularly call for a response. Of late, TVCs have included free telephone response lines where a specific product is being promoted, but this hardly constitutes direct response TV advertising. With the global move toward digital television broadcasting comes an increasing ability to know who is receiving a particular broadcast and for that person to interact with their TV set. Therefore, TV advertising is likely to become more interactive over the next five to 10 years.

Ultimately, the aim of CRM is to communicate and interact with an audience of one. It is vitally important that marketers, and indeed the agencies which support them, bring CRM into the overall media mix used by their company. It is far too easy to pour money into TVCs, as everyone enjoys the glitz and glamor surrounding their production. The key question, however, is: will a TVC reach the person you are really reaching out for?

The following is extracted from a speech delivered in October 1997 by Niall Fitzgerald in his capacity as chairman of Unilever. He was addressing a gathering of the best advertising agencies in Europe, and it really was a wake-up call to the industry. The fact that the speech was given in Europe is irrelevant; Fitzgerald could just as easily have been speaking to any gathering of agencies anywhere in the world.

As we look at the way the world is going and then we look at the traditional advertising agency, we believe we see an alarming discrepancy developing between what our brands are going to need and what contemporary agencies are good at.

To date, the only way to reach our consumers has been through mass media: the same, single television commercial, for example, seen by as many as 50 million people. It's just not possible to be equally sensitive and appealing to the separate needs of each of 50 million different people—or even 50.

Mass communication has its best days behind it. Relationship marketing is the new world. It will be more exciting and more satisfying than the very limited world it replaces.

This speech was significant in that it was the first time that anyone of Fitzgerald's significance in industry had stood up and stated publicly that relationship marketing, or CRM, "is the new world." Unilever is currently spearheading a joint project within the United Kingdom to build a profile of British households, in terms of the products they buy from Unilever, so that it can more specifically target its marketing spend to each household.

Advertising provides opportunities to create "interaction" between the audience and the advertiser, but such opportunities are often missed. For example, print advertisements may fail to include a response coupon or phone number. Response mechanisms can give advertisers an idea of who is interested in their product and be used in building a marketing database. As such, they make their marketing spend (ads) work harder.

With the advent of the Internet, most companies now include their website address in their advertising and marketing materials, so those consumers who have Web access are being given an opportunity to respond or find out more. When you run an advertising campaign, do you include an area on your website for people who visit to leave their details and request more information?

So, CRM is different from advertising. Advertising is just one of a range of techniques available to marketers to communicate with consumers. It tends to be based on monologue and aimed at wide audiences. CRM is based on dialogue, involving customers, and is highly targeted, ultimately to an audience of one.

IS CRM DIFFERENT FROM DIRECT MARKETING?

Direct marketing, at its worst, can involve "cold mailings" to a list of names, sourced from a bureau, about whom the marketer knows very little, other than that they apparently conform to the specifications supplied to the bureau. The marketer has no real idea whether these people might be interested in buying the product they have to sell.

A good direct marketer will segment the list into control groups and try different creative styles and incentives in an effort to find that magic formula which generates the highest response rate. But even the best direct marketing campaigns run in this manner may deliver only a 1% or 2% response. Consumers usually have a negative perception of this type of marketing, because the chances of the product or service being something they need at that particular time are pretty remote. This type of mail-out has rightly earned the label of "junk mail"—because, for most recipients, that's precisely what it is.

Nevertheless, direct marketing has come a long way in the last 20 years, aided by the same technological revolution that has enabled CRM. With more powerful computing, the best direct marketers are able to merge many sources of data in an attempt to refine the targeting of the mailing. But, despite this, response levels remain well and truly in the low single figures.

Having said all this, those direct marketing campaigns that are run by a company trying to sell more to an existing customer can enjoy significantly higher responses to a well thought-out campaign. We have personally run campaigns that have seen percentage responses ranging from the mid-twenties to the low thirties. So, why should there be such a significant difference in levels of response? It should be common sense, really—if you have already bought from a company and you are happy with the product and service, and that company takes the trouble to offer you other products which they know are relevant to you and therefore of value, and at the same time rewards you for responding, why wouldn't you respond? This is a clear indication of the value of the relationship in marketing terms.

If someone you had never heard of asked you out on a date, what is the likelihood you would accept? Compare that with a situation where it is someone you have known for a while, you know you can trust them, and you know something of their personality—isn't it far more likely that, in those circumstances, you would accept the date? Direct marketing is like trying to get someone you have never met to go out on a first date. CRM is more akin to asking a friend out for the evening.

Direct marketing is often used as part of the CRM armory, but it is only when it is used in an intimate way—employing customer knowledge and giving relevant information—that it is really effective, as Case Study 1 illustrates.

Case Study 1
BARCLAYS BANK
Getting personal

One of the U.K.'s largest and more traditional high street banks is heading down the CRM route. At the end of 1999, Barclays Bank announced a new initiative to send a new *Quarterly Update* to its customers.

The *Quarterly Update* takes the form of a newsletter, containing information on all Barclays products and services already held by the customer, as well as specific recommendations on new products the customer ought to consider, and suggestions for improving the way they are currently managing their finances.

The *Quarterly Update* is expected to generate a significant increase in cross-sell activity for Barclays. It provides a perfect vehicle to offer additional products and services to customers, but in such a way that the customer sees the relevance of the product and feels that value is being added to the basic banking service.

Barclays is using new software that enables it to look at the relationship each customer has with Barclays, and to find ways to improve it. A spokeswoman for Barclays explained that "there are hundreds of different recommendations and scenarios that can be triggered, which makes it a highly personalised service."

Barclays piloted the *Quarterly Update* in the East Midlands area of the U.K. before rolling it out automatically to customers fitting the profile of those who were most responsive in the pilot program. Other customers can gain access to the service,

but they must request it via their branch or via the telephone
banking service.

IS CRM DIFFERENT FROM CUSTOMER SERVICE?

The simple answer to this question is that the two are very closely
related, because CRM is all about building brands by giving customers
wonderful experiences. In fact, product and service quality are at the
center of all the great brands. Traditionally, customer service has always
been an important part of brand building for every company, and
especially for service companies. It has offered great opportunities to
companies to get close to their customers, and to build long-lasting
relationships with them.

Unfortunately, many companies have failed to take advantage of
these opportunities and have damaged their brand images as a result.
Instead of leveraging the brand experience by giving excellent customer
service, they treat their customers like irritants. Poor customer service
may range from not listening to customers, or being unable to help them
because someone else dealt with them last time, or being unable to deal
with queries because they relate to a different area, to being under so
much pressure that customers are made to feel unwelcome. We have all
heard about or experienced poor customer service. Each time customer
service fails to delight the customer, it is another nail in the coffin of the
brand; poor customer service rapidly kills brand value. Even the millions
spent by some companies on training their staff in customer service
techniques still only manage to inculcate generic interpersonal skills at
the end of the day. There are the rare exceptions, of course, as Case
Study 2 illustrates.

Case Study 2

PAN PACIFIC HOTEL, VANCOUVER, CANADA
Reading customers' minds

A senior executive from Sun Microsystems, after staying at the
Pan Pacific Hotel, Vancouver, congratulated the hotel's vice

president and general manager, Steve Halliday, on how well his staff could read her mind. This had nothing to do with resident palm readers, astrologers, or fortune-tellers; it was a reflection of the fact that the executive felt she had experienced service excellence.

It's not surprising, because this hotel is very different. A division of the conglomerate Tokyu Corporation of Japan, the Pan Pacific Hotel Group currently has 17 hotels. The president of the hotel chain, Ichigo Umehara, is what we would call a brand champion: he works hard to differentiate his company from the many competitors in the hospitality market. The company certainly sets out to do things differently, and that can be seen from its mission statement, which states that the company wants "to take people successfully to places they have never been before." Staff are called associates, and are empowered to a great degree to take decisions affecting the consumer experience at the point of contact with each guest.

The associates are carefully selected at all levels, and can go through up to 14 interviews with colleagues and management with whom they will be working before being offered a job. As Steve Halliday says, "We always try to hire the best—the 9s and 10s—because if we hire them, they will recruit good people. If we hire 4s and 5s, we'll end up with a staff full of similar-caliber people." The philosophy at the Pan Pacific is to "hire on attitude and train on skills," the opposite of what many companies do. The staff are so happy, they are non-unionized. A recent independent survey identified the things they like most about the company:

- the family atmosphere—it's a home away from home;
- teamwork;
- respect and equality;
- learning and advancement;
- pride in their operation; and
- fun.

These attributes have become embedded values, the culture of the hotel, and they are transmitted to the customers. The hotel chain doesn't have human resources departments. Instead, it has people innovation departments, emphasizing the desire and confidence in employees to excel at innovation. They talk about education, not training, and they call their major functional parts of the business "independent business units" to encourage associates to think beyond being part of a hotel.

The whole idea is to create "emotional links with guests through personalized care." They want the guests to share the "home away from home" feeling they have. Which brings us back to our opening paragraph in this case study. If you think about it, your family and close friends know you well and can anticipate what you are thinking and what you need. They can read your thoughts and feelings, and they try their best to help in every possible way. This is what the Pan Pacific associates do in Vancouver, and the end-result is that customers don't just have a great experience, but enjoy a relationship. So, when customer service excels, CRM lives.

The hotel chain isn't a great brand yet, but it's getting there. Of course, it has invested in technology and software to enable the employees to deliver on the brand promise. The challenge, as with every brand-building initiative, is for the company to achieve consistency in the brand experience across all its hotels. In Vancouver, it really is outstanding, and a prime example of a CRM initiative led by customer service.

Technology plus attitude equals CRM

Traditional one-to-one service hasn't worked for many companies because the service attitude hasn't been in evidence, or because the systems that front-line staff need in order to gain real knowledge of each customer haven't been available. Attitude is a management problem that can be overcome, as we have seen above, but the technology to assist this is now freely available. A front-line employee with CRM technology at his or her fingertips can talk to each customer as an individual, and with confidence, knowledge, and respect.

You will find many examples in this book of how CRM allows you to help your staff do things right. The technology allows for easier, more natural, and less intimidating relationships. For example, CRM programs can give ready access to information on the customer's previous contacts and purchases, enabling staff to quickly get to the heart of a customer's needs and solve their problems. CRM makes everything easier for the consumer. It is redefining the standards for customer service and brand management. While customer service is an exciting and vital part of CRM, in this book we describe how you can achieve a great brand experience with the use of techniques that complement customer service initiatives. Two case studies illustrate this point.

Case Study 3
SMALL BUSINESS SERVICE BUREAU
Pushing power to the point of interaction

The Small Business Service Bureau (SBSB) was founded in 1968 to help small companies with legislative advocacy and with buying health insurance products at group rates. It also began helping large health-care companies with related enrollment and administration tasks, performing the role of a traditional service bureau for their small business customers. "Before we had an integrated call center, each of our agents was trained in just one line of business," says Brian Carroll, executive vice president and chief operating officer of SBSB. "We realized we needed to establish a broader platform for delivery of services to our industry. By making our business call-center-centric, a whole new world of opportunities has opened up to us. Now each agent can handle calls on our full line of products. We're running four different subsidiaries through one call center. The technology is irresistible."

Using Oracle database and applications software, together with customer-interaction software from Versatility Inc. (now part of the Oracle offering), the database and front- and back-end applications are integrated to provide powerful customer solutions. Here is an example of the benefits received by using this CRM integrated approach.

The versatility call-center technology is the foundation for all SBSB's teleservice and telesales activities, giving customer service agents a wealth of information about their customers. As an outbound call is made or an inbound call is routed to an agent, the call center software immediately supplies the agent with the pertinent customer information. With the click of a mouse, an agent can move between customer profiles; product information; customer history; order entry data; fulfillment requests; template cover letters; a quote entry system; callback scheduling; and a screen displaying frequently asked questions and frequently raised objections, along with the appropriate responses. Agents can also view notes from the last transaction performed with a particular customer, as well as historical customer notes. "The call center technology has really opened our eyes to many new ways of doing business," Carroll says, helping SBSB to "drive add-on product sales through better customer event tracking" and become more successful.

Today, roughly 50,000 small business owners in 18 states obtain health insurance from SBSB, and the future looks even brighter, thanks to the company's new information technology infrastructure, and a solid vision for customer care.

Source: Oracle Corporation

When CRM acts as a driver for excellent customer service, we can see that it is not only the customers of CRM-based companies that get the benefits; it is also the companies themselves.

Case Study 4
BENEFICIAL LIFE INSURANCE COMPANY
Getting a single view of the customer

In the United States, Beneficial Life uses CRM products to get a holistic view of every single customer. For the first time, customer service representatives can see from one place exactly which policies a customer owns, when they expire, and what previous contacts the customer has had. This has helped Beneficial Life double the number of calls resolved on first contact from 30% to 60%. The CRM system is also contributing to enhanced levels of service for its agents, by providing a quicker turnaround time on transactions. Better reporting capabilities and metrics illustrate that the average turnaround time on transactions has dropped from three days to two days. Voluntary turnover has dropped from 18% to 12%, reducing the time and expense of training new employees.

Source: Oracle Corporation

SO, WHAT REALLY IS CRM?

Customer relationship management is all about building a strong brand. It does so by creating the right blend of organization, systems, and processes that allow your people to understand your customers as individuals, and potentially to tailor every interaction with a customer to their specific needs. The detailed information your people have about each customer also means that they are going to be best placed to identify sales opportunities from existing customers and therefore to maximize revenues for the company.

Let's explore the term "customer relationship management." Focus on the middle word—"relationship." Forget, for a moment, that we are talking about business relationships. Think about the successful personal relationships you have enjoyed—with your spouse, your girlfriend or boyfriend, or your son or daughter. Think about how these relationships have developed—the length of time it involved, and the amount of emotion you have invested in getting to where you are now. Solid relationships are built around trust, understanding, effective communication, and faith—all of which take time to build and even longer to perfect. Some of us spend a lifetime trying to get it right. But then think of the words you would use to describe those relationships—to borrow a slogan from Chevrolet, you might say they are "like a rock," solid, dependable, durable—all of the things we would love to have in our business relationships with our customers.

Don't forget that, along the way, we may have met people we were very interested in having a relationship with, but who weren't interested in having a relationship with us. This exists in business, too, so recognize it and don't waste time, emotion, and money on trying to make a relationship happen.

Try to apply these simple life principles to growing the business relationship with your customers. Don't try to move too quickly; take some time to find out a bit about your customers. Who are they? What are they trying to achieve—not only from interacting with you, but in their life generally? Find out how they prefer to communicate with you, talk to them regularly, don't abuse the relationship, build their trust, present them with relevant, personalized, timely offers that you know will save them time, money, or hassle—and watch your business grow. This is the heart of a good CRM program.

WHO IS CRM FOR?

We have yet to come across a single organization or business that would not derive real benefits from CRM. If you have customers, either end-customers or internal customers (within your organization), if you take the trouble to get close to them and understand their needs better, you will benefit in a big way and so will they. The outcome will definitely be a win–win situation.

Given that the key driver behind CRM is to identify your best (most profitable) customers and then lock them into your company, this technique can apply whether you have 10 million customers or only one. Indeed, if you are a company that only has one customer, you had better find out what that customer wants from you quickly, because if they leave you, you will literally have no business left to run.

Just a word of caution. CRM, even applied well, is not something that can give impact to your business overnight. Like anything in the world of management, and especially brand building, a lot of hard work has to be invested to get the incredible results that can be achieved. To be sure, there will be a number of positive impacts on the business just from trying to look at your "relationship" from the customer's viewpoint, but the real payback to your business will come over time. However, that payback will be real, and it will be permanent. It will bring your company higher sustainable profits, increased asset value, and differentiation from your competitors.

SUMMARY

Before we move on to the next chapter, let's recap. CRM is a good thing. It allows you to do the unthinkable—to benefit your customer and yourself at the same time. It allows you to understand who your customer really is, what they are buying from you and, more importantly, what they *could* be buying from you, and lets you add value to their life while at the same time increasing your profits. And while all this is happening, you are adding immense strength to your brand, because consumers will be realizing that you are listening to them, understanding them, and giving them what they want. They will trust you, and trust is at the heart of a great brand. Does it sound good so far? In the next chapter, we will show you more benefits that will accrue to you, your company, and your brands when you employ the principles of CRM.

3

Brand-building Benefits of CRM

There are many benefits that CRM can bring to your brand, and these are the focus for this chapter. However, first we will explain the basis of how CRM works, and outline the basic difference between ordinary loyalty schemes and CRM programs. Many companies embark on loyalty (points) programs and think that they are implementing a CRM program. As will be shown, there is a lot more to CRM than just giving customers points to maintain their brand loyalty.

HOW DOES CRM WORK?

CRM works by:

- **Creating a continuous communication loop between your brand and your customer**: This can be telephone-based, face-to-face, by mail, the Internet, or any combination of these. The critical thing is to open communication channels and make it easy for the customer to interact with you.

- **Getting to know the customer**: Use this new-found communication channel to get to know your customer—not just their name and address, but also:
  - Who they are.
  - Who is in their family unit.
  - What they do for a living.
  - What their ambitions are.
  - Their likes and dislikes.

  You can only get this information by asking them directly.

- **Using existing customer data**: You need to look at the information you ought to have already about the customer. Included here would be information such as:
  - How often do they buy from you?
  - How much do they spend when they do?
  - When was the last time they bought from you?
- **Asking the customer what they want from you**:
  - What might they buy from you if only you supplied it?
  - What do they like about your brand?
  - What do they dislike about your brand?
- **Establishing the unlocked potential**:
  - What brands do they buy that are competitors of yours?
  - Why don't they buy everything they need from you, if you offer it?
  - What would you have to do to persuade them to buy more from you?
- **Creating the knowledge**: Marry all the foregoing data together to create the most powerful database in your entire organization. This database will drive every single piece of targeted sales and marketing activity to your customer base from now on.
- **Re-using the knowledge time after time**: Each and every time a customer interacts with your brand, make sure that the person the customer interacts with has the knowledge in front of them, so that they can talk to the customer like a friend they have known all their life. It is this concept of intimacy that really helps in the brand-building process.

The concept of brand intimacy

Knowledge is power, and if you can get knowledge about your customers, then you can really become close to them and deal with them on a one-to-one basis. It is the ability to create this degree of intimacy between your brand and the customer that will lock out the competition and maximize the profit for your company. Remember, "He who knows the customer best has no competition." In practical terms, turning the focus of your brand on to the customer means that you should only be doing things that are of value to your customers. This approach, by definition, encourages you to eliminate redundant processes, products, and services—redundant because they are not wanted by your customers, but are merely there because of corporate inertia. It means concentrating on, and streamlining, all your marketing efforts so that the customer and your brand become one.

By getting closer to, or becoming more intimate with, your customer, you will be in the best possible position to sell them something at the time they need it. You will be their best friend, the person they turn to when they need help, guidance and, ultimately, someone to buy from. This is not pressure selling, but quite the reverse: it is sound brand strategy. And by using your customer knowledge base, you will be putting offers to your customers only at a time when you already *know* they will need you. Your advances will therefore always be welcomed. You are adding value to your brand proposition constantly, and not being a nuisance. Consumers like intimacy, but not intrusion, and good relationship management can make the difference between whether your brand is perceived as a really close friend or an unwelcome visitor.

The following case illustrates how CRM was employed in product development by one of the world's most admired brands, resulting in huge corporate savings and pre-launch sales to happy customers.

Case Study 5
MERCEDES-BENZ U.S.A.
Design and launch of the new 'M' class off-roader

When Mercedes-Benz decided to build its new "M" class off-road vehicle, it decided to launch it in the United States. The head of Mercedes U.S.A. knew that the vehicle would be entering a crowded market, and that the mere fact that it was a Mercedes would not guarantee sales. They would have to try something different.

Mercedes U.S.A. obtained details of all current owners of off-road vehicles and Mercedes cars and entered them on a database. They then undertook a series of mail-outs to the people whose names were on the database.

First was a personally addressed letter from the head of Mercedes U.S.A. It said something along the lines of: "We at Mercedes are in the process of designing a brand-new off-road car and I would like to know if you would be prepared to help us."

Americans probably receive more direct mail than people anywhere else in the world, but it's not every day that they receive a letter from the head of Mercedes asking for their help. There was a significant, positive response. Those people who responded received a series of questionnaires that asked for guidance on design issues such as whether the spare wheel should be outside or inside the vehicle, desired engine sizes, exterior colors, and interior designs.

What is interesting is that, along with the completed questionnaires, Mercedes began to receive advance orders for the vehicle. The customers felt that Mercedes was custom building a car just for them. No other manufacturer had ever involved them in the design-and-build process in quite the same way.

As a result, Mercedes pre-sold its first year's sales target of 35,000 vehicles. It was expecting to spend US$70 million on marketing the car, but by using the CRM, one-to-one approach, its advertising costs were reduced to US$48 million, a saving of US$22 million. We have heard that the program was so successful, Mercedes is looking to use the same approach in the future with other model launches.

THE DIFFERENCE BETWEEN LOYALTY SCHEMES AND CRM PROGRAMS

In their practical application, CRM programs can take many shapes and forms. We will debate in this book what does and does not constitute a CRM program, but it is useful at this point to draw a distinction between a loyalty scheme and a CRM program.

Most people are familiar with, and probably part of, a number of loyalty programs, or points schemes as they are sometimes known. Just about every type of retail outlet in every city in every developed and developing country has a loyalty program. When you buy groceries, you earn points; when you fill up with gas, you earn points; when you fly, you earn points, and so on—hotel stays, car hire, even surfing the Internet now earns you i-points or mouse miles. If it is not points or miles, it is in the Starbucks or TGI Fridays mould of collect six stamps and the next coffee or meal is free.

Points programs such as these are designed to keep you coming back for more, and it is true that they might influence brand loyalty to some extent, although the degree of influence is debatable. Do these programs constitute CRM? Our view is that they do not, but they can certainly provide a solid foundation upon which to build a CRM program. Normally, these programs have a mechanism—for example, a brief sign-on questionnaire—to collect a little data about the customer and their purchasing habits, but all too often they fail to take the next quantum leap that makes the difference and turns a loyalty program into a CRM program. That leap is achieved by capturing that data, turning it into knowledge, and using that knowledge in some way to tailor the product or service you offer that customer to make it more relevant, more suited, and more specific to their needs. Without this customization, a loyalty program is just a process of "earning and burning" points, and although consumer habits may be affected momentarily, competitors can merely offer more points with the result that the "loyal" customers you thought you had disappear.

Research going back as far as the mid-1990s indicates that, generally speaking, points-based schemes do little to improve the loyalty of customers. What the company is not demonstrating is a real ability to listen to the customer and treat that customer individually. Points-based schemes thus tend to be based on monologue, not dialogue. And at the end of the day, they don't contribute to the differentiation necessary to build a powerful brand.

The frequent flyer example

We will illustrate what we mean with an example of a commonly seen marketing initiative that contains elements of both a standard loyalty program and a CRM program. Many of you may belong to a frequent flyer program. A typical frequent flyer program has two sections—one aimed at the economy traveler, and the other at the lucrative "front-end" (that is, business and first class) traveler.

When aimed at the economy passenger, a program typically has an "earn and burn element," which means customers earn points when they travel and, once they have enough points, they redeem them for free flights. The idea is that customers will pick one airline over another on the basis of the accumulation of more points toward their flights.

We have worked with a number of the national carriers, and most of the research we have seen suggests that this type of program has little influence on a person's choice of carrier. Most frequent flyers tend to choose an airline based on convenience of departure points and timetable. These people may have a preference based on in-flight service quality if scheduling were not an issue, but for the frequent flyer it is. Additionally, the standard of service on most airlines is by no stretch of the imagination great, and consequently it is not a key differentiator for most people who have to make multiple trips.

However, from our research we know that what *does* influence people is knowing that if they fly with carrier A, they get to use the express check-in and the executive lounge with free food and drink, they get extra baggage allowance, and they have a pretty good chance of an upgrade. This is where the CRM program starts to kick in.

Once customers have flown a qualifying mileage, they are invited into the upper tiers of a frequent flyer program. Here they will receive a range of program-specific benefits that are designed to make life easier and more comfortable for them. At this level, airline staff are usually trained to be able to relate to each customer by their preferred name and to learn to recognize regular travelers by sight. The best programs are multi-tiered, with a "Chairman's Club" or similar at the very top. Here only the very best customers get invitations to exclusive events, direct lines of communication to the chairman's office, and never have to stand in line for anything.

In the following case study, you will see how the personal touch provided by a CRM program can have a major impact on the customer brand experience, resulting in loyalty and profitability.

Case Study 6
BRITISH AIRWAYS
Building brand loyalty with CRM

British Airways (BA) wants to grow its brand. It has a vision of wanting to be a true world brand. This is a differentiator in itself. While most companies aspire to become the leader in their industry, BA wants to become one of the most elite and admired brands in the world. En route to achieving this, it wants to become "the undisputed leader in world travel," but this is only a stepping stone. BA recognizes where real profitability and asset value comes from—the brand itself. When you consider that the brand name itself can be worth multiples of the net assets of the business, this may come as no surprise, but few companies have such lofty ambitions. BA has made some mistakes in its pursuit of this goal, and is currently sorting out some business problems, but it has pioneered some great service quality initiatives, and its CRM program is one of them.

BA introduced its successful Executive Club in 1991 and is aligned to the "Air Miles" program, so that customers flying on the airline earn air miles. These can be redeemed for free flights, but also count toward progression through from the bottom "blue" tier to the "silver," "gold," and "premier" (platinum) levels. The interesting thing about this program is that BA has found itself the owner of a massive pot of unclaimed air miles, as many people don't bother to redeem the miles they have collected. BA has found that it is not air miles that the profitable front-end travelers seek; rather, it is the prospect of rising up through the tiers of the card program that drives their brand loyalty. And if you think about it, if you spend a great percentage of your time on an aircraft, would you really want another flight as a reward? What these customers want above all is to be recognized for who they are and for their value to British Airways.

Some of the stories we have heard about what the top members of the Executive Club receive by way of service are incredible, but they illustrate the commitment an organization must make in its day-to-day activities to look after its truly valuable customers.

BA apparently have special staff on the ground both at London's Heathrow Terminal 4 and New York's JFK Airport, who are trained to recognize top customers and intercept them before they get anywhere near a check-in line. These customers are then led to lounges where all their check-in work is undertaken.

We have also heard a story of a BA 747 captain on a long-haul flight leaving the flight deck to chat for varying amounts of time with each of the first-class passengers. After talking for quite some time with one particular passenger, he shook hands with him and discreetly handed him a card. While it appeared that the captain was spending random amounts of time with each passenger, in fact it was well orchestrated, depending on which card level the passenger held—the higher the card level, the more time the captain spent talking with the passenger. The person the captain spent the longest time with was the holder of a premier card. What the captain had passed to him was his personal business card, with his contact numbers. These passengers are told, "If there is anything that you are unhappy with during any part of your flight, call me and let me know personally." Within BA, the captain has total responsibility for ensuring that the airline's most valuable passengers have a comfortable and entirely trouble-free journey.

In 1991, British Airways made profits of £130 million. Approximately 90% of its marketing budget went on advertising, with the remaining 10% spent on CRM. By 1997, its marketing budget was roughly 50% advertising and 50% CRM, and its profits amounted to £670 million. By focusing on the customers they already had, by developing areas of service which made high-value customers feel wanted and special, they were able to capture a bigger share of each customer's travel spend, which went straight to the bottom line.

It is important to be able to differentiate between loyalty schemes and CRM programs. Consider how the two types of program might work for your own product or service.

We have talked about some of the thinking behind a CRM approach. Let's now move on to look at some of the hard facts that have been supporting the drive toward CRM.

BRAND-BUILDING BENEFITS OF CRM

There are many benefits to having CRM in a company, and all of them will help you to build the brand image you desire for your company. Some of the most widely acknowledged of these benefits are:

- **Offensive and defensive brand strategy**: You can use CRM to aggressively attract new customers and to sell more to your current customers, or to build a relationship to shield your customers from approaches by your competitors. (See further on this at pages 40–41.)

- **Increased returns on brand investment**: By getting closer to your customers, you will see not only significant sales growth, but also, more importantly, substantial growth in your returns on brand investment. We explore the reasons behind this below (see pages 43–44).

- **Stronger and cheaper customer acquisition rates**: There is no doubt that a customer who feels valued and loved by you will be more likely to remain with you and give you every opportunity to do more business with them. Not only this, but a satisfied customer is normally very willing to provide names of others who they feel will benefit from your products and services. Typically, these leads tend to have a similar profile to that of the customer introducing them, because people tend to associate with those who have similar lifestyles. This is why member-get-member campaigns can be so productive if you focus on your most profitable customers.

- **Increased customer referrals**: This is closely connected to the above point, as your satisfied customers will become the best unsalaried salesforce you will ever have. You just need to know how to harness their potential, and CRM will do this for you. Brand building by word of mouth is very powerful. Companies such as Yahoo! relied on building their brands entirely by word of mouth in the early years, reducing marketing spending and customer acquisition costs significantly.

- **Lower rates of brand defection**: Many organizations are guilty of being so focused on finding new customers, they forget about the ones they have already; consequently, they end up with high levels of customer churn. The single biggest reason given for customers switching to another brand is that they have little emotional attachment to the brand. Emotion sells, and brand defection is a direct result of this, being manifested in consumer minds by feelings of not being wanted or loved. By showing your customers that you care, you can significantly reduce brand defection.

- **Expressing brand personality**: If you demonstrate that, as an organization, you listen to and react to your customers' needs, that you make it easy for them to talk to you, and that you react when they tell you you are doing something wrong, you will be giving a face to your brand that makes it appear welcoming, friendly, and responsive. These are all good things for building the long-term value of your brand. In fact, CRM is a great way to express your brand personality. (See further on this below at pages 42–43.)

- **Increasing staff loyalty**: In the same way that a "happy" customer tends to be a more loyal customer, if your staff are feeling fulfilled you are less likely to suffer major staff churn. There is nothing more frustrating for a staff member trying to service customers than to feel they don't have the means or authority to do what is needed. Removing the "red tape" and empowering staff across a wide range of disciplines can only have positive impact on staff morale and loyalty.

- **More effective use of advertising and promotion budgets**: Sensible reallocation of the A&P budget into "below the line" CRM activity will mean that your marketing messages reach the people you want to talk to, at the time they are most likely to want to buy from you. It makes your A&P budget work for you effectively, and avoids wasted advertising. Spending large sums of money on big broadcast messages is sometimes necessary for high-level brand image statements, and particularly for those brands that want to reach a large mass of people, but when messages are needed to target individuals, it is very difficult to make a rational case for "above the line" activity. It is also not really necessary when you already have a significant database of customers who are ready and willing to buy from you. Unfortunately, many companies don't think about this, and make big costly splashes that reach a lot of the wrong consumers along with some of the right ones. CRM helps you to focus and get more response for your dollars, and to track more easily those campaigns that produce results.

- **Better understanding of the business cost drivers**: Going through the discipline of planning and cost justifying a CRM program can give you a better understanding of some of the key cost drivers for your business. It will help you to uncover the answers to some very important questions, such as:
  - How much does it cost you to acquire a new customer?
  - How much does it cost you to hold on to an existing customer?
  - How much will an individual spend with you, on average, over their lifetime?

  If you don't already know the answers to these questions, you *will* do when you use CRM.

- **More effective, relevant product design**: By getting closer to your customers and opening the communication channels with them, you will be surprised at the amount of information they will volunteer, often unprompted, on things they would like to see you improve in your products or services. This is getting design guidance "straight from the horse's mouth." It will help you to make your brand offerings more relevant to the consumers you are targeting. It also means, of course, that there will be much less likelihood of new product failures. This leads us to the next benefit.

- **Reduced research needs**: We won't make many friends in the research field by saying this, but if you have frequent dialogue occurring with your customers, you can talk directly to them and ask them for specific answers to specific questions. If they feel you are genuinely interested in their opinions, they will turn out for an evening and give you answers to your questions. You will find you have no need to commission pieces of anonymous research when your customers are waiting for you to ask them directly. The valuable knowledge gained from customer conversations can transform your database, enabling you to select customers who tend to buy a particular product or fit the profile of people who ought to buy your product. Yes, it is research, but it is very specific and the responses you get are likely to be much more indicative of what the customer will actually do, rather than what they say they might do.

- **Increased profits and brand value**: The end-result of all the above advantages is sustainable increases in profitability and increased asset value. By increasing your knowledge of your customers and their needs, focusing your marketing spend on customers who you know are more likely to be responsive, while at the same time reducing the rate at which customers defect to your competitors, you will see significant impacts on your bottom line and, consequently, on the value of your brand.

- **Adding value to investor relations**: At the same time as the company is achieving high levels of returns on brand investment, the very fact that the company is so consumer-centric sends all the right signals to your shareholders and other corporate investors. The stature and image of the brand rises exponentially, as the company demonstrates, by its focused efforts in *only* doing those things that add value to consumer lives, that nothing is "wasted" and that the total brand experience is superior to the competition.

We will now cover a few of the above points in more detail, to help you think about what they mean for your business.

Offensive and defensive brand strategy

CRM is both an offensive and a defensive brand strategy. Getting closer to your customers will mean that you will have opportunities to sell more to them, their family, and friends. But the strength of the relationship you can develop means that they are far less likely to be tempted away from you by offers from competitors, *even if the offer being put in front of them is, on the face of it, a better offer.* Maybe it is a case of better the devil you know than the devil you don't, but a customer who is happy with your basic product and service, and who feels you are going that bit further to understand their needs, will generally resist switching to another brand.

Let's illustrate this with a personal experience within the banking industry. A friend's bank in the U.K. is one of the older, more traditional banks. The banking sector in the U.K. is being swamped by newer brands. Some of these are on the high street, but many Internet players are also emerging, promising lower costs, better service, and higher rates of interest. Most of these have at some point marketed to our friend, either directly through mailing packs or by advertisements. But he chooses to stay with his current bank. Why? Some time ago, he was given a personal account manager to manage his and a relatively small number of other people's accounts. The process started off with a single interview, in which the account manager built a profile of our friend in terms of his life to date, his family, his aspirations, his job, his financial needs, and his current financial arrangements, not just with this particular bank, but a total picture. All this information was committed to file. The account manager is now our friend's single point of contact with the bank.

He has since taken out a number of new products with the bank, and the account manager uses the information on file to fill out the application forms for him. The best part of the process is that he is only ever asked for information that isn't already on file, avoiding the irritating practice of many banks of requiring customers to provide basic information anew each time. This service means that the customer doesn't have to fill out lengthy forms, and with data already supplied, it saves time and effort. That is worth more to him than any money saving he might make by banking via the Internet. Who do you think our friend is likely to approach next time he wants another banking product? The brand image of the bank gets a boost every time this happens for each customer, providing a defense against enticements from competitors, and an attack in terms of superior service quality.

Expressing brand personality

We mentioned in Chapter 1 that good branding is all about establishing a great relationship with consumers. In other books (*Branding in Asia* and *Hi-Tech Hi-Touch Branding*), we have outlined what it takes to build a powerful brand, but a significant element of any strong brand is the "personality" of the brand itself. Most of the world's strongest brands are built on brand values that are defined in terms of personality characteristics, because consumers can relate to them and form relationships with them so easily. Defining the brand in this way also makes it easier to communicate with the consumer, because the personality dictates the look and feel of the corporate creative design and the tone and manner of the communications copy. The success of this approach depends on how well and extensively the company applies the brand personality to everything that impacts on the consumer. In service companies especially, this means making that brand personality come to life in every encounter with each consumer.

It is personality that adds the emotional dimension to the brand—its human face. Companies that try to build brands by concentrating on purely rational features and attributes find it difficult to differentiate themselves from the myriad of competitors in the marketplace; they need to establish an emotional association between the brand and the consumers in order to survive profitably. Many famous brands have emotional and rational characteristics as part of their brand personality. Rational characteristics might include "reliable" and "innovative," while emotional items might include words like "passionate" and "caring." Once defined, the characteristics play an important part in how the brand develops its relationship with its customers.

CRM, when executed well, helps every company to express the personality of the brand to each and every customer, and to execute this with the consistency required to build brand acceptance, trust, and friendship. Any communication with a customer must reflect the brand personality, and as CRM is based on dialogue with customers, it provides many opportunities for the company to do this. Therefore, any CRM program must concentrate on expressing the brand as if it were that personality. It is extremely important, therefore, that you define the personality of your brand clearly, as application of this in a CRM context will deliver brand consistency and success. You will read more about this important topic on page 112.

Building brand value—increased returns on investment

Let's start this discussion by referring to the PIMS (Profit Impact of Market Strategies) database at the Stamford Research Institute (SRI) at the University of California. The PIMS database holds over 25 years of marketing and financial data. Each year, 600 of the world's top companies submit their data to the institute. Many of the trends that have affected major businesses around the world over the last three decades have been clearly reflected in the data contained in this database.

In the 1970s, PIMS was signaling companies to focus on volume. In the 1980s, it was signaling them to focus on quality. But since the 1990s, it has been showing that those companies that focus on developing a strong relationship with their customers will obtain twice the sales growth of those that don't. That is a reasonable suggestion, if you think about it. If you form a relationship with your customers and open up the communication channels with them, you are going to be best placed to pick up a second, third, or even multiple repeat sales.

But, here's the shock: those same companies can expect to receive six times the return on equity, as illustrated in Figure 3.1. Just think about

Figure 3.1: The financial benefits of strong relationships

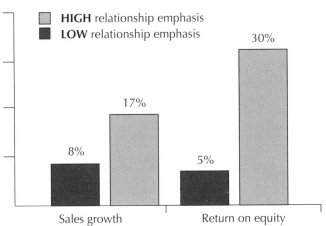

Source: PIMS/SRI

that for a second: *six times the return on equity*. Why should there be this massive return on investment? Well, it has a lot to do with the power of brand loyalty.

BUILDING BRAND LOYALTY

One of the most important benefits that companies look for in implementing CRM programs is the building of brand loyalty. Figure 3.2 looks at the early life of a company or brand, and relates the time to profitability, customer acquisition costs, and brand loyalty. Let's consider more closely what this important graph is saying.

We begin with year zero—this is the point where you are trying to acquire your new customers. Your marketing spend is out there working hard for you, and you will attract some customers. Now, unless you are extremely fortunate, the chances are that you are unlikely to make enough profit from those customers to cover your marketing costs in the first year. Many companies have to wait until the second year before they begin to make any profit.

As time goes on, assuming that you are delivering your products and services to your customers' satisfaction, your marketing can deliver increasing numbers of purchases from your customers.

Interestingly, the longer you hold on to a customer, the less time and

Figure 3.2: The value of customer loyalty

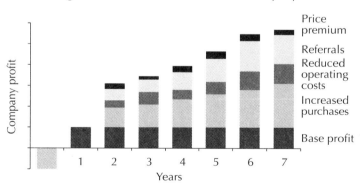

Source: Bain & Co.

money you will have to spend on servicing them. We see this in our work as consultants. When we first start working with a new client, we have to spend a lot of time understanding the customer and their organization, agreeing on working and reporting procedures, and so on. As the relationship between the client and agency builds, we become increasingly comfortable with each other and with our way of working together. There are fewer phone calls going back and forth checking on where projects are "getting to"—all of which adds up to significant savings in time, which goes directly to the bottom line.

Once you have a steady relationship with your customers, they are happy with you and what your brand proposition is, and you have built the trust and confidence so vital to successful brand building, a wonderful thing starts to happen—word-of-mouth referrals. It is often said that an unhappy customer will tell at least 20 people about a bad experience, but happy customers also talk about their good experiences. You may not even know it is happening, but personal referrals are the single most powerful means of promoting your company. Not only is someone being made aware of your product and service, but the new prospect is receiving an endorsement from a trusted friend or colleague. This is a rich source of new business that you must tap into.

The final item on the graph is a "price premium." There is a suggestion that where you have a customer who is entirely happy with what you are delivering, and where you have a strong brand supporting it all, then it is possible to carry a price premium over and above the "normal" market value of your product or service. A good example of this is the retail chain Marks & Spencer. Many people in the U.K. are prepared to pay a premium for Marks & Spencer goods, because not only do they know that the quality is consistently high, but if there is any problem at all, they know they can return the goods and obtain a refund.

As discussed, the process of building brand loyalty begins with attracting a new customer. Many businesses are like a leaky bucket—as quickly as you find new customers to pour in the top, existing customers are falling out the bottom. What would happen to your business if you could slow the rate at which existing customers fell out of the bucket? The answer is you would see a substantial increase in your company profits, as shown in Figure 3.3.

Figure 3.3: Reducing defections by 5% boosts profits by between
25% and 85%

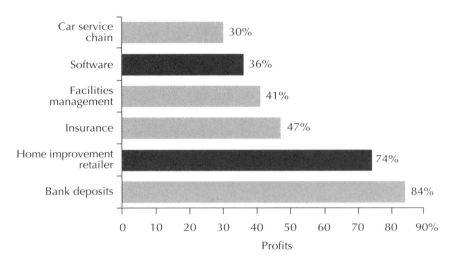

Source: Bain & Co., Relationship Marketing International

Reducing brand switching

When we consider the undeniable economics of focusing on retention
and development of current customers, it is puzzling to find that most
companies are obsessed with going after new customers.

Even the old marketing textbooks will tell you that it costs five or six
times as much to acquire a new customer as it does to retain an existing
one. Many companies find it impossible to show a profit in the first year
of trading with a new customer, because of high acquisition costs—so
why do they still have sales teams that focus on looking for new
customers? While they are focusing on finding those new customers,
their good, profitable, existing customers are walking away from them.
Figure 3.4 explains why.

The main reason customers leave is that no one is talking to them,
so they don't feel valued or loved.

Insisting on customer dialogue

Let's go back to our human relationships analogy. Many relationships
end because one partner was so busy looking at other talent, they forgot

Figure 3.4: Why companies lose customers

Customer moves away or dies	4%
Competitor wins customer over	5%
Lower prices	9%
Poor handling complaints	14%
Lack of attention or interest	68%

Source: TARP

to appreciate and cherish the partner they already had. You might remember an old song by Rupert Holmes called "Escape" (the Pina Colada song)—if you've never heard it, search it out. It tells of a husband and wife who had let their relationship become stale. He places an advertisement in a personal column for his ideal woman. He gets a response—a perfect match—and they arrange to meet. Guess who turns up? His wife.

The moral of the song is that if you don't talk to your customers regularly, you won't be able to understand what they want and expect from you, and they won't feel valued and loved. In fact, the chances are that they may be responding to someone else's advertisement right now.

So, begin a dialogue with your customers now, especially the most profitable ones. Leave them in no doubt that you are interested in their well-being, that you value them, and that you are there to help them.

Now that you understand the fundamental need to look after your existing customers, we will give you another reason for doing so: customer advocacy.

CUSTOMER ADVOCACY—THE POWER OF WORD OF MOUTH IN BRAND BUILDING

If you look after your current customers well, by consistently meeting or exceeding their expectations, they will become your single most powerful salesforce.

For the last 20 years or more, American Express's most powerful sales tool has been its member-get-member campaigns. Yahoo! also relied heavily on word-of-mouth customer advocacy in the early days of its phenomenal growth. It didn't bother with advertising; instead, it let its satisfied customers establish brand awareness for them.

The great thing is that if you select your most profitable customers and ask them to refer you to a friend or relative or colleague, there is a very good chance that they will refer on someone who has a similar social, financial, and personal profile as them. This means that the new customers gained in this way are likely to provide similar profitability, the reason being that people tend to associate with people of a similar demographic and psychographic profile to themselves.

Once you have established an ongoing dialogue with your customers, brought together your internal knowledge of which products and services they currently buy from you, and talked to them to increase your knowledge of them as individuals, of their life ambitions, of their family, and of their possessions, then you are ideally placed to begin to sell other products and services to them. But make sure that you undertake this very carefully.

It is important that you only offer products and services that you *know* will be useful to them—that will add value. If the customer perceives no value in your offer—that it is not relevant to them—it will be filed in the junk mail bin. It is only in the area where your offer overlaps with their needs that any real value will be perceived. The trick is to maximise this area of overlap, and that means harnessing and applying all your knowledge about them. Doing this will add value to your brand, as shown in Figure 3.5.

Adding value to your brand really means that it has to do one of the following:

- Save the customer money.
- Save them time (time equals money).
- Save them hassle (offer a quicker/more efficient service).
- Be customized specifically to their needs.

Figure 3.5: Adding value to your brand

Increasingly, it is this last area that is becoming the focus of attention for most consumer-centric companies. They are employing their new-found knowledge of their customers to "tailor make" their product or service offering to specifically fit the needs of one specific customer. This is commonly referred to as mass customization.

It may be that they offer more choice of the basic product. For example, Honda launched their market-leading CBR 600 motorcycle in two versions, one for standard road use, and a second, the Sport, for those customers who want to take their bike on to the race track and therefore tend to make substantial alterations to the standard bike. The Sport has stronger valve springs, and a removable engine management chip to allow for race exhausts and highly tuned engines. It also has a number of weight-saving measures, including removal of the center stand. By tailoring their bike for two specific customer groups, Honda have been able to build something that has a much greater brand value for each group.

It may also be that by using the latest technologies, a company can offer a product that is entirely tailored to an individual customer's exact requirements, from physical products such as Levi's jeans, bicycles, and swimsuits, to softer service-related ideas, such as Singapore Airlines enabling first-class passengers to choose their own meal, and the exact time they would like it to be served during the flight.

One question you ought now to be asking yourself is: "How can I put my customer in charge of the design of my product or service?"

The time famine

It is likely that most of the customers who fall into your "profitable" or "very profitable" categories will be people with very full lives. Most of these people have money, but what they have very little of is time. If you can save this group of customers time, it is as good or better than saving them money. We refer to this phenomenon as time famine. As we progress through our lives, the more successful we become in terms of our careers and family, the more demands are made on our time. As we move through the 21st century, this will become an even worse problem.

Look at Figure 3.6 and see how many of these time famine factors you can relate to. If you can relate to them, then you will inevitably have customers that relate to them too. Can you help them to overcome the time famine?

Here are some good examples of "added value" aimed at ordinary people who have very full lives and no time to spare.

Figure 3.6: The time famine

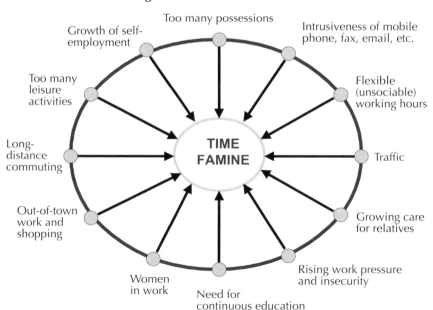

Source: Relationship Marketing International

Airlines: Self/telephone check-in

Many of the major airlines and airports now have machines that allow you to check yourself in, if you only have carry-on luggage. This means not having to stand in line at the airport. Those of you who are frequent business flyers will know that standing in a line with just a briefcase, waiting to check in for a morning flight behind a tour party of 20 people who invariably have communication problems with the check-in clerk, doesn't make for the best possible frame of mind to meet a client at the other end of the flight!

For business travelers, telephone check-in means that they can ring up and check themselves in. They can then arrive at the airport closer to their departure time, which means they have more time to do what needs to be done and less "down time" waiting around at the airport.

E-banking

Whether you are happy about it or not, the Internet is here to stay. Financial services is one of the areas where more people have concerns about using the Net, but once you have begun e-banking, it's hard to see how you managed without it. Being able to sit down at your computer after dinner and pay credit card bills, set up direct debit instructions, and transfer money between accounts is liberating. The reality is that you now have a 24-hour banking day. You are now empowered to manage your own money, and as one of the U.K. banks points out in its advertising, e-banking customers are now all bank managers!

Clothing

Have you discovered the wonders of no-polish shoes and non-iron shirts yet? Of course they don't mean exactly what they say, but you certainly have to spend less time maintaining them. Every little bit helps.

Online grocery shopping

For most of us, the weekly visit to the supermarket is a chore we would rather do without. Many of the high street stores are now offering Internet users the ability to log on, order your weekly groceries, and have them delivered to your door. Not only that, but if you have items that you need regularly, you can just tell them how often you need them delivered and you only have to order them once. What could be easier?

Florists that go that bit further

The more switched-on florists now ask you not only who you are sending flowers to, but why you are sending them. If they are for birthdays or anniversaries, they then make an entry in their diary to contact you next year at the same time. Not only do they ensure that you don't forget an important occasion, but they also get the best chance of your business next year, and the year after.

What very specific added-value products or services could *you* be talking directly to *your* customers about, customers whom you already know have little free time and are interested in labour-saving ideas?

4

Organizing for Brand Management and CRM

GOOD BRAND MANAGEMENT NEEDS CONSUMER FOCUS

For brands to be successful, there needs to be a total shift toward consumer-centricity. In other words, the consumer should be the sole focus for all brand initiatives. So whether it is the website, product development, advertising, the CRM program, or anything else that will influence the brand image, all activities have to reflect the brand *consistently and appropriately*. In many cases, this means that companies have to change their structure to make it easier to be close to the customer, and with CRM this is usually inevitable. In this chapter, we will take a look at how you might re-shape and refocus your organization to be able to deliver the brand experience of your product or service, tailored to individual customer's needs and values.

The organizational impact of heading down the CRM route cannot be over-emphasized. It would be easy for us to pretend that that was not the case and lure you into a false sense of security. However, particularly if you are working within a major organization, this is a major piece of work that requires a major piece of thinking. For smaller companies, of course, it is somewhat easier, but corporate reorganizations are always traumatic experiences both for the organization and for the individuals working within it. They always meet with resistance because, as we have all been told many times over, people don't like change. You will need to approach this sensibly, but never forget that the results will be worth it. You can build an outstanding brand in a very short time.

MAKING YOUR BRAND CONSUMER-CENTRIC—CHANGING MINDSETS

Let's start by looking at what you are trying to achieve. Your current organization is probably aligned to different product areas or distribution channels—that is, it is product-centric. This is a traditional model and one that has evolved for quite sensible reasons, based on the way business was done in the past. Many companies in many industries, including telecommunications and financial services, are used to operating in this way. Indeed, even in the newer hi-tech industries, product-centricity abounds. Stan Shih, chairman and CEO of the Acer Group, refers to this syndrome as a company being technology-centric, and says that the computer industry, in particular, has always emphasized products more than people.

A product-centric organization will think from the inside out, asking questions such as: What skills do we have? What are we good at? What raw materials do we have? Having got the answers, they then develop products that they think people want, find ways to distribute those products, and promote them via advertising and special offers in the hope that consumers will buy them. Figure 4.1 shows how this looks diagrammatically.

This type of mindset, cultivated by many organizations, gives rise to the "ivory tower" syndrome, where the vast majority of people are so far removed from a living, breathing consumer that they cannot possibly have the best interests of their customers in mind when they are at work.

Even the concept of having a customer can seem alien. We have witnessed a manager of a management services unit in a major financial services company stand up in the question and answer session at the end of a "customer care" workshop and state, 'All this is fine and good, but

Figure 4.1: Thinking from the inside out

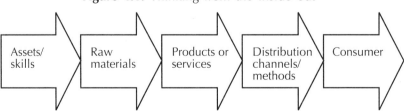

I don't have any customers.' It's easy to see how ridiculous that statement is, but that type of thinking is rife within many major organizations. The point is that *everyone* has a customer. That customer may be an end-consumer, but they could also be someone who receives a service from elsewhere in the organization, maybe even from someone within their own team.

A paradigm shift in management thinking

In any company that wishes to create a powerful brand, each manager must constantly ask the question, "Who pays my salary each month?" If the answer is "My boss" or "My company," he or she should go straight to jail and not pass "Go." The only correct answer to that question is, "My customers."

So, the key question for every manager every day is, "What am I doing today to add value to my customers' lives?" Managers who realize that it is customers who are putting the money in their pay packets usually have an appetite for getting to know those customers better. After all, the more they can do for them, the more money is likely to end up in their pay packets. This is not a new marketing methodology; it is basic economics.

Changes in structural thinking—the inverted pyramid

Here is a slightly different approach to illustrate the need to become consumer-centric. We have all heard about how progressive companies have inverted the management pyramid, by going from having the boss at the top and everyone supporting him or her, to having the front-liners at the top and the boss and other managers supporting the whole team. You can see the idea in Figure 4.2. If we bring consumers into the frame and draw in the point of attention at each level, you will see why "old-style" companies have such a major challenge on their hands. As shown in the pyramid on the left, everyone is facing into the company, and no one is looking at the poor old consumers. Companies that take consumer-centricity seriously, like those depicted in the pyramid on the right, focus all their efforts on consumers and empower their people to give them a good brand experience.

Figure 4.2: The inverted pyramid

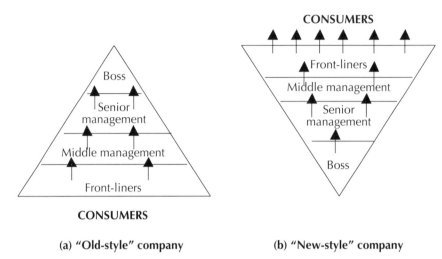

(a) "Old-style" company   (b) "New-style" company

The consumer-centric organization

Acer's Stan Shih has consciously been shifting his company's thinking from technology-centric to consumer-centric. He has repositioned Acer, stressing this to internal and external observers with the slogan, "Acer, Bringing Technology and People Together." A consumer-centric organization thinks from the outside in. Everyone in the company is there to support the generation of customer delight, so the typical organization pyramid inverts. Once companies start to put the customer first, and start to think from the outside in, then the process takes on a completely different look, as shown in Figure 4.3.

You can see what a fundamental change in thinking this can be, and how right it is, but it can be tough for people to begin thinking this way. For the company to really operate in this manner, many people are going to be taken way out of their comfort zone, but it has to be done for the

Figure 4.3: Thinking from the outside in

| Consumer needs and wants | Consumer channel preferences | Customizable service/ product offer | Raw material requirements | Required skills and assets |

good of the consumer and their own futures. "No pain, no gain" is a phrase that applies to corporate as well as personal fitness. The companies that have developed the most powerful brands have done so by always thinking from the outside in, starting with a thorough understanding of what consumers need, want, and feel.

Norwich Union, a major U.K. insurance company, was previously a wholesaler of general insurance products, retailing mostly through third-party intermediaries. This created a substantial degree of remoteness between the brand and the end-consumer. Norwich Union used to have a brand that boasted "No-one protects more." This was typical of a large company tag line aimed at competitive differentiation that wasn't translated into a brand experience that showed real customer concern. Like many of the companies that rely on agents, distributors, or other intermediaries, the brand experience was out of the company's control. And when that happens, not only does service quality slip, but the equity of the brand erodes as well. This is why many other top brands, including prestige retailers such as Gucci, have or are buying back their franchises so that they can once more control the brand experience.

Having recently merged with Commercial and General Union, another major U.K. player, in mid-2000, Norwich Union has emerged from a re-branding exercise proclaiming "Together we're stronger," supported by images of its happy customers going about their daily lives. This is a significant attempt to turn the focus within a company of 8,000 people away from themselves and firmly on to their customers. Norwich Union has won a number of industry awards in recent years for its customer service initiatives, and it is heartening to see a giant company such as this attempting to become intimate with customers once again.

Enter the customer manager

Some of the most powerful brands in the world have major organizations based around product, with brand and product managers being the most important people in that structure. But they are changing, and so can your company.

In this new-style company, it is not the brand or product manager who is most important, it is the "customer manager." The product managers become effectively suppliers to the customer manager. To enable this paradigm shift to take place requires managers who understand the importance of customers, who will listen to and believe what customers are telling them, and who will track and constantly monitor each point of interaction with the customer to make sure their company gets it right each and every time.

It is essential, then, that each manager is given responsibility, not for a range of products, but for all aspects of delivery to a selected group of customers. Look at the way management responsibilities have changed in companies such as Tesco, the supermarket chain based in the U.K. For years, the store manager's key responsibilities were the day-to-day store operations—making sure the shelves were stocked, that the delivery orders were placed, and so on. Now, this is all delegated activity. The store manager's prime focus now is getting to know each of the store's highest-value customers by name. Each store manager makes phone calls on a regular basis to ensure that their highest-value customers are happy with Tesco. Is there anything they have done to upset them this month? What could Tesco be doing more of? Why? How? Tesco has realized that these top customers represent 80% of the store's profits, and that if any of them are unhappy and take their business elsewhere, Tesco's profits will be walking out of the door at the same time and the value of the brand name will decrease.

CUSTOMER SEGMENTATION AND OBJECTIVES

Segmentation

Segmentation has always been a key element of any marketing strategy and is vital to the branding process. The better defined the target, the more effective your brand strategy is likely to be. How you segment your customer base is, to a degree, up to you. There are no real right or wrong answers to this. Customers can be broken into segments based on a whole range of variables, and in the past companies have concentrated on a whole range of demographic and psychographic variables. Your company will need to decide which is the most relevant to its situation, but the key ones as far as CRM is concerned are very different to the traditional methods of segmentation. Instead of concentrating on the age, sex, lifestyles, and other variables that can be used to segment target populations, CRM-based companies are more concerned with elements such as:

- the present value of their customers;
- the potential lifetime value of their customers (if they remain loyal to the brand);
- the number of products their customers currently hold, and could hold;
- the frequency with which they buy their products or services;
- the customers' preferred means of contact/distribution (walk-in, e-commerce, telephone); or
- any combination of the above.

Customer profitability, which is what CRM companies are really seeking, tends to be a product of lifetime value, frequency of purchase, and product holdings.

Objectives

Whereas a traditional product manager would be given product development objectives, the new-style customer manager will be given specific objectives to meet for their allotted group of customers, such as:

- Increase the average number of products held per person to 3.0 from 1.2.
- Increase the overall value of the customer group by 25%.
- Increase the size of the group by 10% by finding more customers with the same profile.
- Reduce the attrition rate within the group of customers to 3% from 15%.

There are more, but you will immediately notice that there is not one mention of total volumes or total numbers of transactions in this list. The focus has changed.

What is also noticeable is that every one of these objectives is capable of measurement and tracking. Some companies may face a few challenges with IT support because their systems may presently be built around product divisions, and they may need to pool data from a number of sources before they can then extract the view they want and need. In fact, many business processes need to be revisited in order for a company to make itself more consumer-centric.

REVIEWING YOUR BUSINESS PROCESSES— SPRING CLEANING

As part of the move to your new customer-centric organization, you will need to undertake a complete review of the business processes which support the organization, to ensure both that there is a sensible flow of data and that important customer information is available at all points of interaction with the customer. This is a great opportunity to undertake a bit of "spring cleaning" by critically reviewing each of your business processes, starting at the customer and working back into the heart of your organization.

Frequently, in going through the exercise of mapping the process, overlaps can be identified in the form of costly process duplications, or areas where streamlining can occur to deliver a more efficient service to the customer and a more cost-effective delivery for your company. This is part of the technique commonly referred to as business process re-engineering, and it's an important component of a thorough CRM installation. Typical questions asked in reviewing business processes are:

- How many tasks are being performed each day within your company which add no real (measurable) value to either your customers or your organization?
- Why are they there?
- Does every step add something to the process? If not, does it need to be there at all? Each step you can remove will not only save cost (and therefore increase your profitability), but will bring the inner parts of your organization one step closer to the customer.

Once a company begins to look at its business from the outside in, rather than from the inside out, it can begin to understand the key areas it should be focusing on—those areas that have the highest degree of interaction with the customer, or that deliver those parts of the service which the customer sees as a priority. The end-result is a brand that customers appreciate and value.

Sony appears to have embarked on a global CRM initiative. Both in its business-to-business and business-to-customer operations, Sony seems to be grasping the nettle and getting closer to its customers. That such a hi-tech, innovative company as Sony should invest in CRM solutions is a fantastic endorsement for CRM and its importance to major brands. Sony is using CRM techniques across its businesses to build its brand image. The following case study documents its initiatives in the business-to-business arena. (Case Study 17, in Chapter 9, looks at Sony's business-to-consumer initiatives.)

Case Study 7
SONY (INDIA)
Case history

Sony is a brand that is known universally for its hi-tech, highly innovative products. However, prior to this initiative, the customer experience in trying to order Sony products and parts in India was anything but hi-tech.

The problem

Sony (India) has a sales and service network which comprises:

- 33 distributors
- 1,400 dealers
- 85 authorized service centers

Each of these business partners is key to Sony being able to manage the overall customer relationship. Ensuring that finished goods and spare parts are being made available efficiently is key to maintaining the Sony brand image.

Previously, the process required much manual intervention. Orders were submitted to sales executives, who would "bundle up" orders before they were submitted to Sony's CRM system from SAP. This could build in delays of anything up to 24 hours. Sometimes, when a sales executive was not around, orders simply could not be placed at all. In addition, sales executives, in interpreting the customer's order, had a tendency to guide orders toward products they wanted to sell, rather than those the customer actually wanted.

The authorized repair centers fared particularly badly, as they were heavily dependent on timely ordering and receipt of critical spare parts. The only way to order spares was via email, fax, or post. There had been problems with orders not being recorded at all, or processed incorrectly, and lead times for spares were at least three days.

The solution

Sony needed a hi-tech system for their customers. They elected to extend their internal SAP system to customers via the Web. The system now allows customers to go online themselves and place orders for goods and spare parts directly on to Sony's system. This has had a number of positive impacts:

- Delivery time has reduced by at least one day.
- Customers can now select the exact product or part they want.
- Customers can track the status of their order through the system.

Sony has also made a number of new facilities available to their business partners:

- It is now possible for customers to see their accounts with Sony online.

- They can view an analysis of their sales performance for a given period. This can help them to track the impacts of sales promotions and discounting.
- They can view online updates on Sony's products, as well as full technical details.

For the authorized service centers, the new system means immediate order placement, as well as the ability to track availability of critical spares across Sony's storage facilities in Delhi, Mumbai, Bangalore, Chennai, and Calcutta.

By providing this level of system support to its business partners, Sony is projecting an image of a company at the leading edge of technology, as well as one which is keen to empower its business partners, many of whom will also be working with other brands. It is important, therefore, that Sony builds confidence and trust in its partners, as well as making Sony a company it is easy to do business with.

Source: SAP and Sony (India)

Systems—risk versus reward

One of the biggest challenges will be to change the style of systems supporting your business. Most of the "off the shelf" systems that are available are product-oriented and have limited amount of customer function. Software companies are beginning to bring products to market that will give you the information you need—but, as you well know, you can only get out of a system what you put into it in the first place.

The tradeoff with the emerging systems is balancing the extra risk of using an unproven system against obtaining the benefit of the latest functions. For example, many IT departments in major organizations will tend to shy away from the first release of new software and wait for later releases which tend to have fewer bugs in them.

In the world of CRM, there are many new releases of software from many different origins, as it is an evolutionary process. It is best to sit down with the IT director and understand what your company's position is on this. This will give you an idea of how radical you can be with your systems proposals, and IT staff can help to evaluate the alternatives.

Learn to work together

The next challenge will be to get teams who have been trained to look after their own profit centers to begin to work together physically and financially for the good of the overall company.

The drive toward more accountability for individual departments is laudable—we believe very strongly in financial accountability—but the unfortunate side-effect is that teams can suddenly become very uncooperative in helping one another if they are going to incur costs and thus exceed their budgets.

There are two strategies you should adopt to overcome this. First, make sure that a manager who has enough seniority in the organization to manage team conflicts champions the CRM project. This is necessarily a general manager, or even the CEO. Second, create a mechanism that ensures that these teams don't just incur cost, but will also benefit from the extra revenue and profit generated by the CRM program. Costs are easily seen, and you will have to do a bit more work to ensure that the incremental revenues for each department can be recognized and reported.

Start with a pilot program

Often, to prove the financial worth of any CRM activity, it is necessary to set up a pilot program and monitor its impact. Most of the highly successful CRM programs have begun on a relatively small scale, and have subsequently evolved to become bigger and better. Tesco's "Clubcard" program, for example, started off in 1994 as a pilot that ran in only four stores. Once the pilot was deemed successful, it was rapidly rolled out in 1995 across the entire national store network.

Running a pilot is a great way to convert "non-believers." Build your own mini-case study, look for some early, quick wins—some positive impacts—and then feed that into your financial case for a full-blown CRM installation.

This leads into an interesting area. Where a number of divisions are becoming involved in your CRM pilot and each has a marketing

Figure 4.4: A multi-department approach to CRM

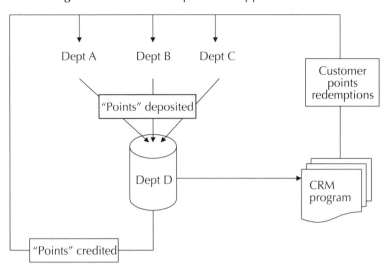

function and marketing budget, how can you take a single customer view and manage the cost and reward mechanisms? One answer is to let one department take the lead.

Establish a lead department

This approach makes one department responsible for the administration of the CRM program, and that department acts as a kind of "clearing bank" for the points. Figure 4.4 illustrates how this might work.

Take four departments within an organization—departments A to D. Each one wants to participate in the corporate CRM program, and department D is elected to administer the scheme. Each department first must decide how much of its revenue it can afford to invest in the CRM program. This need not be constant between the departments, and realistically is unlikely to be, particularly where the products or services provided by each department are of significantly different values or have differing profit margins.

To pay for the cost of this administration overhead, one option is for department D to make an internal management charge at $x\%$ of the value of points being accrued and redeemed within the scheme. This can, in turn, change a marketing services department, previously seen as an overhead, into a profit center! Of course, this should not be your motivation for such a move, but it is a sensible way of managing an essential support function for the pilot program.

As you move forward from pilot to full program, you will be reviewing your entire organizational structure and supporting systems in any event, but you may well find that this arrangement will survive into the new system.

OVERCOMING "ROADBLOCKS" TO YOUR CRM PROJECT

There are a number of reasons why, despite your best efforts, the progress of your CRM project may become frustrated. The most common reasons we have come across are:

- lack of budget and resources; and
- lack of buy-in/understanding of the project.

Lack of budget

Budgetary constraints could be an issue, but a properly constructed financial case for a CRM program is likely to show that it won't take long to get the investment back, and over time the return on investment will be many-fold. It doesn't take much to balance the books in terms of incremental sales, especially if the focus is on high-value customers.

We have found it useful to put together a simple spreadsheet that at least makes a reasonable attempt at a cost justification for the project (see Chapter 7). It might even look at just a pilot running of the CRM project. Typically, the spreadsheet would list the costs that will be incurred in running the pilot. It would also look at how many people are needed, systems development costs, and the costs of creating and printing documentation—letterheads, brochures, envelopes, postage— and cards (if the intention is to give out a loyalty card). A budget would be included for a launch event and, perhaps, promotional incentives. And, most importantly, if loyalty points are going to be given away to customers, these will need to be accounted for.

The best way to approach this is to decide on a notional points value—for example, 1 point = $1, or 100 points = $1. This is the dollar value that you will put into your accounts, as points are allocated out to customers, and as they are redeemed for other goods and services. When you set the dollar value, you need to think of the practicalities of applying the value within the CRM program. This needs to be set at a sensible level, and you will need to find a balance between not having too low a value and customers collecting millions of points, and not having the value too high so that it seemingly takes forever for people to amass any volume that they can redeem for tangible rewards.

Reality checks

Having detailed the costs, you need to begin to work out where the incremental revenue will come from to offset the costs and, hopefully, generate some positive income for the company. To do this, you will need some reality checks.

First, think about what you are trying to achieve with the CRM program. You want to open a dialogue with your customers in order to find out more about them, their friends and family, so that you can personalize the service you give to them and therefore be perceived as adding more value to their lives. In other words, you are trying to build up the total brand experience. The other reason for this dialogue is to identify not only everything your customers are buying from you currently, but more importantly, all the things they *could* be buying from you. You are, in effect, creating a marketing plan for each and every one of your customers.

The "top down" financial view

Now, what do you feel might be a reasonable estimate for the increase in sales you might expect—5%? 10%? Break it down further—to what percentage of your customers do you think you could sell more of the current product or service, or a better version of your current product (up-selling), or a different product or service (cross-selling)?

Another way to view the program is to estimate the financial impact of losing the business of 10% or 20% of your good customers, and then look at the relatively low cost of investment to defend that business. Odds on, it will look like a cheap project!

Now look at the number of customers you are going to involve in the pilot, multiply that number by your average income per customer, and apply your increased sales estimated percentage. Are you breaking even?

The "bottom up" financial view

Sometimes it pays to work the other way. Take your projected costs and divide them by the number of customers you are going to involve in your program. Now look at what percentage increase in sales you need to achieve per customer to at least offset the costs. Does it make sense? This is most likely to be the view your financial director will take of your numbers, so it is good to be prepared!

These are all good reality checks—it is easy to get carried way with plans for expensive launches, brochures, and plastic cards—but ultimately it has to stack up financially. It will do the world of good for the project's credibility, to say nothing of your own, if you have completed this groundwork in advance.

When you have to compete for budget and resources with every other "pet project" in the organization, being able to demonstrate financial contribution can only help your case. Bidding for budgets and resources can often be like applying for a job. Prepare yourself well, do your groundwork, and present your paperwork (c.v.) in a clearly laid out and concise manner. In the same way that a recruitment manager will breathe a sigh of relief if your c.v. is legible, complete, and easily digested, so will your CEO when faced with a number of bids for money from the corporate pot. If you are thorough and clear in presenting your financials, you will give yourself the best possible chance of success.

Lack of buy-in/understanding of the project

The other thing you must not neglect is the internal marketing of your project. We don't apologize for returning to this and want to emphasize the point that the harder you work on internal marketing, the better chance of success you will have. You need to raise the profile of your project whenever you can. Take every opportunity; each casual encounter by the coffee machine or in the car park with a member of your peer group or your manager is an opportunity to talk about what you are setting out to achieve, or how things are progressing. Divide and conquer! Engineer opportunities—put a brief presentation together which you can deliver at a team meeting or use to illustrate your project whenever you talk about it. You will win supporters.

To assist the in-house marketing process, you may wish to consider producing a brief newsletter, which can be circulated regularly to teams that are key to the success of the project. We have used this with great success a number of times—it is a great and fun way of ensuring that everyone knows that you are still there and what you have managed to achieve so far.

Reusing current initiatives

One of the pockets of resistance you may find for your project may well come from individuals or teams who have begun internal initiatives that are related to loyalty or cross-selling. These may be projects they have been involved in for some time, to which your project may appear as a threat. This feeling can be heightened when you are using an external agency. A common reaction from managers of other projects is, "Why should these 'outsiders,' who know nothing about our business, think they know more about what we need to do than us?" This is the illogical, but emotional response that is quite likely to surface. Even involving the opposition in your project may not turn them around to be on your side. As with any major project in a sizeable organization, politics will, at some point, come into play.

Emotions aside, there are sensible reasons to have a good look around your organization for initiatives that may be taking you in the right direction. These may form important building blocks for your project and, if you are really lucky, enable you to fast-track part of your delivery. This means you can be quicker to market and save costs at the same time. Of course, if you do manage to bring these pre-existing initiatives within your project, you stand a better chance of bringing some of the skeptics along with you.

Finding champions

We have often found that there are a number of frustrated customer champions being suppressed in organizations—they have all the right ideas, they know what they need and want to do, but they are unable to find support for their thinking. Determine who these people are and let them see that they can use your project as a vehicle to put some of their ideas into place. Not only will they become your strongest supporters, but they are also likely to have done a lot of the thinking already and can steer you around the speed bumps. Let's face it, this is what good consultants do best—it is why companies engage them in the first place, and it's what gives rise to such jokes as "What's the definition of a consultant? A person who asks you if they can borrow your watch and then tells you the time." That is often the perception. The reality is that you had the watch all along and no matter how long or hard you stared at it, you couldn't read the time. Consultants have a role to play, but the real problem is that many people don't know how to use consultants effectively. It is a sad reality of life that the message conveyed to your senior management team from an external consultant may well succeed, when the same message from an internal team may be perpetually challenged.

Some years ago, a friend was working at a large insurance company, where he was heading a team that put together one of the company's first five-year business and IT strategies. At the same time that this project was running, a separate business process re-engineering project was initiated within the company, spearheaded by a group of IBM consultants. Our friend's project had already facilitated a number of workshops with the company's general management team and had drawn up a first-draft strategy. There was some resistance to the approach his team was proposing, which was seeking to put the focus more heavily on to the customer and away from functional divisions. This was radical thinking for this company, and his team was having a tough job selling it to the project sponsor.

The IBM team, who had been told about the work of our friend's team, took away the project files and looked at the groundwork as part of their work. At first, the internal team was a little put out—this was *their* hard work, and *their* pet project, and they weren't too happy about the IBM people potentially using their ideas. But the reality check was that, there was no glory for the team in continually having their ideas and suggestions rejected. They knew in their hearts that their ideas were the right ones—exactly what the company needed—but they hadn't managed to convince management. The IBM consultants agreed with what the team were saying, took their suggestions and put them on to IBM stationery, and presented the result to the senior management team, who bought it. Did the in-house team lose out? They didn't think so. Having spent six months burning the midnight oil, they were happy to have their ideas approved. The moral of the story is, of course, learn how to use consultants to your advantage.

THE QUICKEST ROUTE FROM HERE TO LAUNCH

Once you have made your financial case and obtained the resources you need to get your project under way, you will find yourself under a lot of pressure to show quick results. Senior management are never the most patient people on earth, and once you have dangled the carrot of additional sales and profits in front of them, they will be keeping a close eye on the progress of the project and will be eager for results.

Outsourcing as an option

If you try to pull together all the skills you need internally, you may find it difficult to get under way quickly. Have a good think about outsourcing. There are specialist companies that you can plug into to handle much of what we call the "donkey work." There are many companies that can deal with activities such as:

- data entry;
- data preparation;
- creative/studio work;
- print production;
- warehousing of documents;
- letter shopping (personalized letters and mailing packs);
- fulfillment (stuffing envelopes and despatch); and
- call center for assistance and queries.

Using external resources can be costly, so, wherever possible, obtain competitive quotations from several companies.

Migration strategy

While your pilot is running, think positively about how you are going to implement the full-blown program at the end of the pilot period. To be able to present a truly customer-centric organization, you need to go through a process of staff retraining and fundamental restructuring. How do you approach this, and maintain and improve your service to the customer, while going through a period of corporate turmoil?

There are two possible solutions. One is to "hide" your organization behind an external call center. You can use the call center to provide an apparent single point of contact, and let the call center operator negotiate the way through your reorganization, rather than the customer.

The other approach would be to set up a "model office" within the company. Take a select group of staff from each of your core disciplines and bring them together into a new team. Provide them with the telephony and systems they need to be able to handle most types of day-to-day sales and service transactions and let them be the window into the organization. If you need to prioritize whom they should service, look after your higher-value customers first.

We have covered a lot of the ground concerned with what kind of things you need to do to make your CRM efforts successful, but we also need to point out that unless you position your CRM initiative properly, there may be a possibility of failure.

HOW TO POSITION CRM IN YOUR COMPANY (THINGS TO WATCH OUT FOR)

More often than not, it will be the marketing department that promotes the idea of devising a CRM program for a company. It is likely that marketing will be the department that a CRM consultancy will approach first, and they are therefore likely to end up "championing" the project internally.

Be warned: this can be the top of a very slippery slope. Many of the problems encountered when installing CRM programs stem from being designed in the "ivory tower" of marketing and then imposed on the operational areas. This is when the NIH ("not invented here") effect kicks in. Even though the program may be conceived by, and likely championed by, the marketing department, it is typically not the marketing department that "touches" the customer each and every day.

A well-applied CRM program is like a thread that runs through the entire organization. So, whatever department actually takes responsibility for driving the program, every division, every department, and every staff member must know about the program, its objectives, and, most importantly, what their role is and how they contribute to the running of the program. It is for this reason, as we will later explore further, that the internal marketing of the program is just as important as the external work.

The importance of internal communication

It is advisable to launch an internal communication exercise at the launch of the *project*, not the launch of the *program*. Take, for example, a retailer. The marketing department may design the best loyalty card program in the world, but if the staff on the shop floor don't know of its existence, don't understand it, and cannot promote it to the customers in-store, then it will never succeed. If the card is used without the correct point of sale systems in place, the data won't make it through to the marketing department, and they won't be able to give the customer the rewards they have earned. So, IT department buy-in is also critical. This will only be achieved if the IT department understands not only *what* system they have to build, but *why* it is needed, and *how* it will contribute to the welfare of the business.

The reality is that the only way to install this type of program is with the complete understanding and cooperation of every division of the organization. Involve them in both the design process and the installation process, and you will attain buy-in. These comments are based on numerous practical experiences of well-conceived and well-intended projects which would have delivered great benefits to the customer and the companies involved, but which barely made it off the drawing board before being "buried" by organizations which, for whatever reason, just didn't "get it." The hard-learned lessons from these experiences demand that you have the support of *all* the key senior managers, that they back up their words with actions, and, above all, that your project champion/sponsor has enough influence to be able to drive it on over any speed bumps which get thrown in the way.

The following case illustrates the value of internal communication and staff buy-in to a CRM program.

Case Study 8
Internal CRM in a retail store

We will emphasize throughout this book the need to market your project and program internally, to ensure that you get buy-in within your company. The very best CRM programs we have been involved in have also created a variant of the program focused on staff.

We worked with a retail store in Asia that already had a customer loyalty program in place, but its usage was low—less than 5% of all the transactions in the store were on the loyalty card. When we investigated, we found that the staff didn't really understand the CRM program and weren't really interested. They were reluctant to talk to customers to promote the program in case they were asked a question they couldn't answer. And so the program, which had been a major investment for the company, was gradually dying on its feet.

We analyzed the situation. The CRM program itself wasn't bad. There were some really good benefits for customers, and by working with the client we improved these further. The communications to the customer needed more attention, but communications to staff were non-existent, and we were interested to find out why this was the case. When we looked at the terms and conditions of the program, what do you think we found? The very first condition read: "<company name> staff may not become members of the loyalty program." Is it any wonder that staff weren't interested in the program? Not only this, but if they were in the program, they would have first-hand experience of it in practice and feel much better equipped to answer customer questions.

We worked with the company to create a separate version of the program, *just* for staff. Of course, relevance was important, and it was recognized that some of the benefits weren't really appropriate for staff, so we replaced them with things that were.

We created a staff newsletter specifically for the program, giving details of numbers of members joining each month, total membership, and new benefits being launched, and created a monthly award for the staff member who recruited the most new members.

We built a comprehensive training program, and we let staff train each other. They acted out role-plays responding to some of the trickier questions. (We gave them pocket-sized "crib-cards" as a safety net.)

When we re-launched the program, things went skyward. Within the first 12 months, the average store was achieving percentages of turnover on the card in the mid-20s. The best store was into the 40% range.

The message here is that companies should never underestimate the importance of involving front-line staff in building and running a CRM program. Quite simply, it can be the difference between a major success and dismal failure when you are trying to build up your business and grow your brand.

There is another positive by-product of this whole process. When your staff are better placed to deal with customers and therefore can make them happy, and when they receive positive benefits and recognition for doing so, you could well see your rate of staff turnover reduce, as our client did. This, in turn, means lower recruitment and training costs, all of which have positive impacts on your bottom line.

Furthermore, happy staff will demonstrate a more customer-friendly face for your business, which in turn will keep your customers coming back; it's a virtuous circle. There is no doubt that an internal CRM program will increase the emotional projection of your brand, and put a little bit of romance back into the brand–customer relationship.

THREE GOLDEN RULES FOR STARTING A CRM PROGRAM

To conclude this chapter, we would like to summarize the three main things that must be borne in mind by anyone setting out to build and introduce a CRM program. They are:

- Develop clear objectives.
- Make things easy for the customer.
- Be realistic.

Develop clear objectives

You must have very clear objectives for the CRM program, financial and otherwise, but particularly financial. Ensure that everyone understands what you are setting out to achieve and buys into it *before* you begin, otherwise you are doomed to failure. Your first marketing job is therefore to your colleagues. Getting them to buy into your ideas, and showing them what benefits will accrue as a result of the program, are essential prerequisites for success.

Make things easy for the consumer

When designing a CRM program, don't get carried away with its design without thinking about its use in practice. For example, if your CRM program is points-based, it must be easy for the customer to understand the program to begin with. For example, they must be very clear as to what is expected of them, how they earn points, how they redeem points, and what their points translate into in real terms. If the program gives customers too many hoops to jump through to get the prize at the end, they just won't bother.

Be realistic

Finally, any CRM program needs to be realistic. CRM is not an overnight panacea for all financial ills; it is a major commitment for an organization—and for the *whole* organization, not just the marketing department. Payback can take anywhere from six months to a year. But what needs to be remembered is that a CRM program is a strategic initiative that will make significant contributions to the company over the long term. Like any major brand-building effort, it is a long-term but highly lucrative investment.

If you follow these three golden rules, and always "think customer," the CRM program will help to build a brand that not only your customers will be proud of, but one that will also motivate everyone in the company.

5

Building Brand Value through Customer Profitability

So far, we have discussed the rationale for CRM in brand building, and looked at some of the practicalities and realities you must face when installing a CRM program within your organization. But what form should that program take? In this chapter we will give you a few pointers toward a sensible scoping of your program and how you might structure its application.

When building up your brand, it is important to understand exactly who are the customers propelling your brand to greater heights. This means looking at your customer base in detail, and understanding where the value attributed to your brand is coming from. Essentially, it means deciding who are profitable customers, and who are not.

UNDERSTANDING YOUR CUSTOMER BASE

In planning your CRM program you need, first of all, to build an understanding of the profitability segmentation of your customer database. CRM can be an expensive undertaking—it is an investment you make in your customers to obtain a bigger payback over time. But why spend money where there will be no return on your investment—that is, on those customers on whom you are currently making no profit, or even losing money? You *must* establish the profitability of your customers. If you only have product profitability information currently, then this will be an interesting by-product of your project and may well be an eye-opener for you.

We are constantly amazed by the sheer number of companies who aren't clear about which customers they are, and are not, making money from. Year on year, they continue to pump marketing money into media which they believe are reaching their target audience, but without really understanding what constitutes a "good" customer.

Take time out to get inside your customer data. It will pay dividends. Look at your data through single dimensions first. Look at where your customers are geographically, by age, by income—all of the usual demographics that you probably have some data on. Next, begin to answer some of these questions:

- When was the last time each customer bought something from you?
- How often does each customer buy from you?
- What is the average amount per transaction for each customer?
- What is the total value of money each customer spends with you each year?
- How much profit do you make from each customer each year?

This last area is very interesting; indeed, it should be the metric you home in on, as it is the one you most want to influence. When you analyze your customer data based on profit contribution, you will find a significant segmentation.

Back to Pareto

Time and time again, the Pareto principle has been proven to apply. Figure 5.1 shows that when you investigate the profitability of a base of customers, it is very likely to be true that 80% of the profits come from perhaps less than 20% of customers. It is also likely to be true that a smaller percentage will be responsible for a significant chunk of that 20%. We have even seen companies where 5% of customers are responsible for 90% of profits.

This being the case, do you know who these customers are, and what you are doing that is special for them? If this profile were to apply to your customer base, 90% of your current profits could be under threat if you were to lose just 5% of your current customers. Of course, the trick is to find out *which* 5%.

Figure 5.1: The 80:20 rule

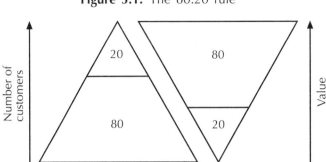

If you were to plot the profit that you make from individual customers, it is very likely that it would look like Figure 5.2.

We have seen a company trying to apply CRM programs blindly to an entire database of 800,000 customers, because the management thought it needed a loyalty program and more cross-selling. Not only is this a major financial commitment—in terms of the cost of customer collaterals alone, without even beginning to consider manpower, systems, rewards, and postage—but trying to manage and fulfill this number of customers is also a logistical nightmare.

When we asked how many of these 800,000 customers were profitable, there was a deafening silence. The point is that implementing a CRM program is a major strategic and ongoing commitment, and has to be undertaken with a sound financial justification and a solid plan. There are two questions that must be considered by any company:

Figure 5.2: Profit distribution

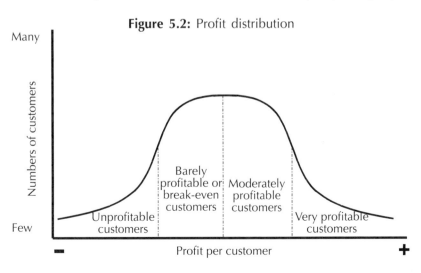

- Why spend money on customers you already find it impossible to make profit from?

- Why spend money talking to customers who bought one product from you two years ago, and to whom you have been unable to sell anything since?

We all know that the marketing budget is hard-won these days. Financial controllers can be hard to convince that your marketing programs are anything other than a cost that they would like to minimize. So, your money should be seeking out customers who:

- buy from you regularly;

- have bought from you recently;

- are making a significant contribution to your company profits;

- are recommending your product or service to friends/colleagues; or

- have significant development potential.

How can you judge what a person's development potential is? We will come to that later, but first have a look at Figure 5.3 which deals with customer profitability. Study the diagram for a moment. You can use it to create an action plan to attack your customer base, and help it to grow more profit and build more value for your brand.

Figure 5.3: Actions to increase profitability

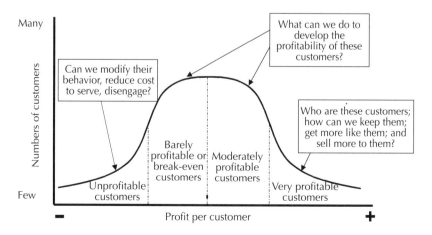

Marketers talk about growth from your existing customer base as "organic growth," so think of your current customer base as a garden. It is a fixed size for the time being, you have limited money you can spend on it, and you want to make it the best it can be. Where do you start? Start with your very profitable customers. These are your prize exhibits. They have grown really well and given you a good show. They are worth nurturing to ensure they have the best chance of repeating their performance next year. In the long term, they are also likely to produce similar high-performing offspring.

On the other side of your garden, you have the very sickly-looking plants. You have spent time trying to help them along, but despite all your best efforts they are not showing signs of growth, let alone blooming. You really have to take a decision as to whether they are worth any more of your time, or perhaps you need to take the hard decision to dig them up and make way for new plants that may well have more to contribute.

In the middle ground, you have a large number of plants that are doing fine, but nothing special. The challenge here is to find the quickest way to bring them on. Do you have the same plants in the middle ground as in your prize exhibits? If so, why aren't they growing as well? Is it the soil? Is it the amount of light? Is it what you are feeding them? A gardener will go through this kind of analysis, and you must do the same. Only by truly getting to know each plant (in your case, customer) can you hope to help your garden reach its full potential.

PRIORITIZING YOUR CRM ACTIVITY

So, stepping away from gardening and back into the wonderful world of marketing, you need to build a profile of your most profitable customers: who they are, where they live, what they do for a living, their family background, and their lifestyle. You may find that several different clusters emerge within the group, but don't assume that they will all have similar traits.

You should concentrate your efforts on the most profitable customer grouping first, for a number of reasons. First, this group represents a significant proportion of your profits, and your first priority must be to defend that profit. Second, customers falling within this group will be priority targets for other companies. If you think in terms of credit cards, these are likely to be platinum cardholders or even higher. They will probably receive more mailings trying to tempt them away from you than any other group on your database. Third, they are spending more than any other customer, so you have most to lose if they go, and we have little doubt that they will give you your highest return on investment if you convince them to stay.

For your next priority, look at the group of moderately profitable customers. Who in this group fits the profile of your most profitable customers? What are they doing differently that means they are not so profitable for you? How can you use your marketing skills via CRM to change their habits and make them perform like your most profitable customers, and therefore increase your overall profitability? This is your next richest source of value, and so, for the time being, everyone else can wait.

CUSTOMER PROFILING

In this book, the refrain that you will come across time and time again is: get to know your customers better. You may be unclear, however, about how to build a knowledge profile of your high-value customers.

First, use the data you already have to build the beginnings of an individual customer profile. As we have said before, you may need to pull this data together from a number of different systems. Once you have performed your stocktake of the data you *do have*, identify the information you would *like to have* about the customer, and then identify the gaps.

How do you plug those gaps? If this were really difficult, you would have a reasonable excuse for not having done it before. Here is the secret: *talk to your customer*—face-to-face, by telephone, by questionnaire, by any means available to you. But start talking to them, and do it now! We have found that customers are usually very responsive to requests for information about them, *provided* they know why you need it, what you intend to do with it, *and* that you will treat the information with respect.

Many of the clients we have worked with have been nervous about asking customers for what they perceive as sensitive information. However, people generally like the fact that you are taking the trouble to talk to them, and they like to become involved. Remember TARP's findings, set out in Chapter 3 (see Figure 3.4): the single biggest reason why customers leave companies (68%) is that no one talks to them—they don't feel wanted. Just taking the trouble to involve them might be enough to hold on to them, without having to give anything else. What a great investment!

Be prepared for an unexpected wealth of "free" information in response to your direct questions, but also a flood of information about what you are doing badly, and what you could be doing for them. This is free research obtained from real people, giving you real data, and it is worth its weight in gold.

STARTING YOUR DATA GATHERING

The hub of any CRM initiative must be your marketing database. Without it, you cannot hope to harness the information you hold about your customers.

In Chapter 2, we pointed out that by using their database effectively, major organizations are able to behave like a small shopkeeper. Small shopkeepers have to develop an intimacy with their customers that not only promotes loyalty, but allows them to keep close tabs on the needs and wants of their customers so that they have the best chance of fulfilling them.

The marketing database

This all makes absolute sense, but the problem is in the application. Most major organizations have data coming out of their ears, but it is held in many different systems, on different platforms, with not all of it current and some of it incomplete. If this sounds like your situation, linking everything together to create a single usable marketing database will take some effort; however, the asset you create in the process will be well worth the time and money invested.

Don't be surprised if your IT department groans at the prospect of the undertaking. They will definitely groan if you try to bring together data from 800,000 customers in one pass. It is advisable, therefore, to focus initially on high-value (HV) and medium-value (MV) customers, prove the process and systems with the smaller numbers, and then consider any roll-out from there.

If you cannot get any joy at all from your IT department—they may simply be overloaded, or their estimated cost may be too much for your pilot project's budget—fear not, because it is perfectly possible for you to set up and manage all the data you need on a PC with a proprietary database product such as Microsoft's Access. You just need to find someone who can build the database for you, and then undertake some basic analysis work once you have populated it.

Segmenting the marketing database

Practical rules

As we have already discussed, all customers are not equal in terms of their value to you; thus, they don't all necessarily deserve the same level of attention or even the same pricing. The implication of this, we have argued, is the need to divide customers into convenient groupings, or segments, to allow us to define a marketing and communications approach for each segment. It also means that we can define specific goals and objectives for each segment and then track the impact of various marketing activities on each grouping.

In Chapter 4, we discussed ways in which you might segment the database, but a good place to start would be based around the relative value of each customer. This at least makes sure that you are devoting your efforts to the customers who are most important to your business. Within this segment, you can create smaller segments based around some of the individual customer profitability metrics, which we will come to shortly.

How big should the segments be?

There are no hard and fast rules governing the optimum size for a segment. The best rules to go by are commonsense ones, created by your resource and budget constraints. The more highly segmented your database, the greater the level of ongoing analysis work you will have to undertake, and the more complex and costly your communication program—assuming that you want to tailor the communication into each segment. The old systems adage of "Keep it simple" is good sense to begin with. Start with a small number of segments and divide from there. Look for clear distinctions between groups.

There has been discussion in various books and publications about creating "'segments of one." This is supposedly the ultimate goal of a one-to-one marketer—but is it? Just think about it for a moment.

CRM and the segment of one

We have heard many observers state that Internet companies are already able to market one-to-one. This gives them a significant advantage over a marketer using more traditional media to communicate with the customer. It is undeniable that the Internet has the capability to make one-to-one marketing easier to apply. Many websites "require" the customer to provide their personal details before they are able to access service over the Web. This means that a prospect or customer record can be created from virtually first contact. In Mom and Pop store speak, it means that no one can walk into your store and out again without you at least knowing their name and contact details. Many websites also use "cookies" to "mark" you, so that if you come back through the door, they can welcome you back by name.

Further, some sites may give you registration or customer numbers. You are then able to do things such as customize your particular area within the site. For example, as a registered reader of the *Daily Telegraph* or other national newspapers online, you can create your own personalized copy, containing only the types of articles you are interested in reading.

Being able to "recognize" a customer in this way opens the door to mass customization—one of the goals of the one-to-one marketer, and so the Internet cleverly creates a degree of self-segmentation. By searching out a particular site, the user is declaring an area of interest. If you were able to track an individual's movement around the Net, you would quickly be able to build an invaluable profile to use for your marketing efforts. We say "if," but of course software already exists that can do this.

Communication over the Web, in many ways, poses exactly the same set of "problems" as any other form of tailored communication. It is certainly true that the Internet has the potential to allow highly personalized responses, as well as electronic marketing to become more and more customer-specific. For example, customers are able to specify if they want to receive their emails as plain text, or include HTML to provide graphics. They may also be able to define the frequency with which they wish to receive mailings. For those that hate "junk mail," typically it is a lot easier to include and remove themselves from mailing lists via an email.

Generally speaking, though, the Web seems to have the ability to make people nervous. Many sites appear to "take control" of the computer, and won't let you go back to where you came from, or spawn windows that you never asked for. To the average user, it can feel a bit like "Big Brother is watching." What appears to be lacking in the Web currently, which must be fundamental to customer intimacy, is the feeling of trust. Very few people in life choose to become intimate with people they don't trust. The challenge for companies courting customers over the Web is therefore to create a feeling of security, confidence, and trust as early as possible, such that the barriers can come down and the relationship building can commence.

In Chapter 9, we will discuss a brand-new dotcom company that has recognized this need and created a number of mechanisms to address it from day one.

Back in the physical world, it is more difficult to market to a segment of one, as that "one" is a living, breathing person who you need to get to know and understand. A *segment* doesn't ring up your call center, or come into your store, or fly on your aircraft; a *person* does. We agree that the ultimate objective could well be to have a highly personal relationship with each individual customer, a relationship which ensures that you know as much about them as is practically possible and allows you to custom-build the package of products and services which you offer to that one individual. The problem with terms like "segment of one" is that they dehumanize the marketing function—which is exactly what CRM is in the process of reversing.

Ignoring the argument over terminology, imagine you have 800,000 customers on your database—do you honestly have the ability to review each of these customers individually? And then to create an individual marketing strategy for each customer? We doubt it. In any case, it is not really necessary. There is enough commonality for you to be able to create a much more manageable scenario than this. For example, Tesco's CRM program, one of the best that we are aware of, which is backed by several years of highly detailed customer performance data, only has around 100 segments within a customer base of nine million; and while it may not be unique, it is probably highly unusual in working to that level of granularity.

If you are in the process of starting up a CRM program in the physical world, then our advice is not to worry about this argument now, but start simply. Find four or five key segments—perhaps segment by spending initially. Look at features such as lifestyle or life-stage within these groupings. Over time, as you compile more data, you can begin to look for more specific groupings. But work within your limits and within what is sensible.

INDIVIDUAL CUSTOMER PROFITABILITY METRICS

We mentioned earlier the term "individual customer profitability metrics," but what do we mean by this? There are a number of features about individual customers that have a direct bearing on their current value to you, and which, if you can influence them, will positively impact on their future value. These features are capable of measurement, so you can track their performance over time. Each one is therefore a component of computing the "lifetime value of a customer." Let's look at these key metrics now.

Value

How much is a particular customer spending with you each month, each year, and ultimately over their lifetime? "Customer" can be defined as one individual, or a family grouping, or, of course, a business if you are working in a business-to-business context.

Frequency

How often does that customer make a transaction with you? How often does the customer stay in your hotel, or hire a car from you, or shop in your store? If you are a grocery retailer, a customer who shops at your store every week might be a great customer. If you hire cars, it may well be someone who rents from you once a month. If your business is a hotel, maybe once a quarter is the average frequency. You need to look at your own business, and work out what constitutes a typical customer transaction frequency.

Recency

When was the last transaction with this customer? This is a very important area to monitor. If you have a customer who buys from you every month and then doesn't order for two months, your customer management software ought to be flashing lights and ringing bells so that you proactively contact the customer to see if there is a problem. Don't expect customers to ring you and tell you that you have upset them and they are not going to do business with you again, because most people just walk away. TARP's research shows that only 4% of customers complain; the other 96% never bother. Of those 96%, somewhere between 65% and 90% will take their business somewhere else next time they make a purchase, and nearly all of them will tell many of their friends. This will do your brand image no end of harm.

Make it easy to complain

So, make it easy for your customers to complain. Don't feel that having a high rate of complaints is necessarily a bad thing for your company. Many of these situations are recoverable if you show that you value their business enough to want to put things right. It is frequently said that the loyalty rate of a customer who has needed to complain to you, and for whom you have satisfactorily rectified matters, is significantly higher than for a customer who has never complained. Why? Because you have at least talked to each other, and you have had a chance to demonstrate that you are interested in them. You have listened to what they want from you and you have reacted. CRM is this simple. All you need to do is encourage the customer to talk to you in a non-complaint situation, and for you to listen and react.

Dormant customers

There are a number of reasons why previously active customers can fall dormant, and it doesn't necessarily mean that you have done something wrong. It may just be that the person's circumstances have changed and they no longer have need of your product or service If this is the case, you should understand this, because no matter how much you spend on marketing activity, the reality is they might not need you anymore. The answer, therefore, is to talk to customers and find out what they think, and whether or not they are still interested in your brand.

COMBINING THE CUSTOMER METRICS

Each of these metrics can give you a good deal of information about which customers appear important to you. But when used in isolation, they could give you a distorted picture. Take a grocery store, for example. Imagine that you analyze the *frequency* with which customers visit your store. You find that 20% of customers visit your store once a month or less; 60% visit the store, on average, every 10 days; and 20% visit the store, on average, every three days. So, those customers who visit your store every month or less are the low-value customers, those who visit every three days are your high-value customers, and the 60% who visit every 10 days are your medium-value customers, right? Well, not necessarily. If you add in the *value* dimension, you may well get a different picture. Your "low-value customer," who visits your store only once a month, may suddenly become one of your best customers. Why? Because they find shopping a chore, instead of shopping every few days, they buy a whole month's worth of groceries at one time. Not only that, but they are a family of six and they buy three trolleys worth of goods at a time. Conversely, those people who visit your store every three days may only be popping in for a pint of milk and a loaf of bread. So, who is the high-value customer now?

When you think in these terms, it starts to raise questions about the merits of the "express checkout" lanes which many supermarkets have put in place. What are they saying to the customer? If you only have a few items, we will help you to get out of the store quickly—but if you have just spent your life savings with us and have two trolleys full of groceries, you will have to stand in line for 20 minutes? Does that make sense?

When working with retail clients, we have taken a different tack by installing fast-track checkouts that are only available to loyalty cardholders. The checkouts are opened whenever the store becomes busy, and provide a quick way out for the most highly valued customers. This is the way it should be. Going back to our Mom and Pop store, customers with loyalty cards are the equivalent of the person who lives in the village and always shops at the store. They are the real valued customers. The non-cardholders are just passing though the village and decide to try the store. Why should they get the same, or a better, level of service than the loyal customers? Not only does this create a real incentive for customers to apply to join the loyalty program, but it enables the retailer to gather a lot more data about who regularly visits the store and what they purchase. In our experience, the percentage of customers who elected to participate in the loyalty program grew from less than 5% to as much as 40% in some stores.

Have a look at your data through these varying dimensions. Build a picture such as that shown in Figure 5.4.

Figure 5.4: Customer profitability metrics model

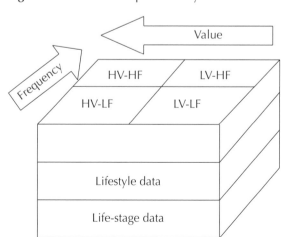

Start by modelling the value and frequency dimensions. This will give you your four high-level segments. Then overlay these with the lifestyle and life-stage data to create the beginnings of a very powerful CRM model.

The segments you will want to focus on are:

- Priority 1: High-value, high-frequency customers.
- Priority 2: High-value, low-frequency customers.
- Priority 3: Low-value, high-frequency customers.

The low-value, low-frequency group holds no attraction for you.

You must defend groups 1 and 2 at all costs. Although they are already giving you a large proportion of their custom, try to encourage them to do more. It is the customers who are coming to you regularly but spending relatively little that present the biggest growth potential. So, it is group 3—low-value, high-frequency customers—that has the greatest potential for your marketing efforts. You just need to find out what they could be buying from you, and what you need to do to get them to buy. By analyzing the lifestyle and life-stage data, you can build a picture in your mind of who these people are. If your lifestyle data is weak, undertake a communication exercise with your customers. Send out a short questionnaire and find out what you think is missing from your knowledge.

Take a look within your high-value, high-frequency segment, and find people who have the same lifestyle and life-stage profile. Find out what is different about the low-value group. This will give you a good starting point. You must then create a marketing program that will influence and provide an incentive for the low-value group to begin behaving more like the high-value group. Case Study 9 describes the CRM program used by Concourse Securities to better understand its customer base.

Case Study 9
THE CONCOURSE SECURITIES CO.
Understanding your customer base

The Concourse Securities Co., established in Taiwan in 1996, deals in stocks and shares.

At the time the company was formed, the securities market in Taiwan was worth 30–40 billion yuan. Within seven months of its launch, Concourse Securities achieved profits of 17 million yuan before tax. However, the company was facing strong competition, and there were a number of key areas it had to address in order to grow:

- How to hold on to its current customers.
- How to grow the volume of business from its current customers.
- How to develop online trading customers.

CRM techniques were employed, with the help of CRM software company AKuP International Inc.

Concourse began by analyzing the data they already had about their current customers. They looked at customers' frequency of purchase, recency of purchase, and their overall monetary value to the company.

Pareto strikes again

Remember the rule that 80% of your profits come from only 20% of your customers? Well, in Concourse's case, analysis revealed that 93% of their total revenue came from only 20% of their customers.

They began to look deeper into the data and were able to build a profile of their most profitable customers in terms of which stocks they tended to buy, how old they were, what number of shares were normally bought, and even which salespeople they tended to deal with!

Concourse's CRM program

Concourse implemented a CRM program which focused on its very best customers, but which also looked to improve attrition rates on other customers.

Priority treatment for "VIP" customers

VIPs are an exclusive group of customers, selected because of their profit contribution to Concourse. VIPs are identified from the moment they contact Concourse, either via the telephone or the Web. They receive priority treatment, personal advice on their investments, and a refund on their brokerage fee, based on the value of the customer. VIPs receive courtesy calls post-sale to ensure that they are delighted with the service they have received.

Developing the value of other customers

- **Proactive customer sales contact**: Concourse developed software with a set of rules that made recommendations to customers on stocks to purchase, based on their previous history. The process works a little like that at Amazon.com, where customers are recommended books based on authors they have previously bought, or the type of book they tend to read, or even those books which people like them have previously bought. A real-time notification procedure was developed so that each day, the customer is contacted with stock recommendations. The contact is via email or telephone, at a time selected by the customer.

- **Tracking customer preferences**: Concourse put a logging mechanism on the website of its investment consulting alliance partner, so that it could learn the preferences of its customers. It also provided a "pop-up" window with a personalized recommendation to the customer from Concourse's portfolio. Any customer who is interested is linked through to the Concourse website so that they can purchase the stock.

- **Outbound telephone calls**: Concourse installed a program of outbound telesales calls to try and build the value of customers who fit the profile of the VIP customers but were still providing low volumes of business.

Counting the benefits

Among the many benefits accruing through this CRM initiative were:

- The rate of refunds to VIP customers decreased from 0.3% to 0.1% of revenue, generating an increase in gross profit of 5%.
- Customer satisfaction rates within the VIP group increased from 65% to 90%.
- Revenue from the VIP group increased by 25%.
- The rate at which Concourse lost its VIP customers was reduced from 10% to 5%.
- Customer satisfaction levels outside the VIP group rose from 60% to 65%.

Source: AKuP International Inc.

DESIGNING YOUR CRM PROGRAM— TIERING

"Tiering" is a term used to describe a loyalty or CRM program that has multiple levels. The levels are normally direct representations of the high-level groupings that have emerged from your segmentation exercise. Each tier will typically have a descriptor such as "premier," or if your program has a card attached to it, you might relate to labels such as silver/gold/platinum. The label offers an indication to the customer that he or she belongs to a particular group.

There are several reasons for tiering, which can be either customer-driven or internally driven:

- **For the customer**: Tiering can provide the customer with a sense of recognition. It says that they are valued and that they have achieved a certain status. In some markets, notably the Asian markets, status is still very much alive and kicking, and is an incredibly powerful incentive to be harnessed by your marketing initiatives. When used to represent status, tiering gives your brand a prestige label, and that can multiply the value of your brand rapidly.

Prestige and status are universal traits among human beings, and are to be found in all markets. For example, British Airways' Executive Club thrives on the inherent snobbery of the British. (Did we really say that?!) BA's gold card tags are valued far more highly by club members than any number of hard-earned air miles. They make a certain statement in the same way that the chauffeur-driven Mercedes-Benz that whisked them to the airport, and the Rolex watch on their wrist, do.

Understanding what drives people in your market primarily, but within your target segments specifically, is critically important to the success of your program.

We worked with an airline recently that was reworking its front-end (first and business class) reward program. These customers are medium- to high-value and regular users of the airline. We wanted to understand their lifestyles in more depth, to understand what might motivate them to make the airline their regular first choice. To gain this understanding, we ran a number of small discussion groups, and some of the insights we obtained were priceless. What would motivate these people to travel more often with the airline? Air miles for free travel? Not really, for the reasons we explained in Chapter 3. Did they want more benefits when they were traveling? Again, not really—there were a few areas where they felt things could be improved, but generally they were pretty content.

So, what was the insight that made us go, "Wow!"? It was when they said, "You know, we're all very busy people. We're successful in our jobs, which means we spend a lot of time at the office, and traveling from place to place. We like to be recognized and looked after when we travel, but we expect that from any airline at the prices we pay. Rewarding us with points/air miles is all well and good, but if you really want to reward someone, then reward our families. We spend so much time away from them with our jobs, if we knew that by traveling with you our families would benefit in some way, that would be a good thing." When we explored that further, they said things like, "If I flew a certain number of miles with you and you rewarded me by giving my family a new TV set, they would really like that." We could have brainstormed a marketing program in the office for months and never have come up with that insight.

Get close to your target customer groups. *Talk* to them, and more importantly, *listen* to them. If you ask your customers questions, you *must* listen to their replies, no matter how unpalatable their response. Otherwise, you might as well save yourself the time, effort, and money! Involve your customers in your program design and you won't go wrong. Indeed, you will create something powerful and rewarding for everyone.

- **For the company:** Giving the customer the ability to aim for higher tiers in a program gives them an inherent motivation to perform in a certain way. By cleverly constructing the thresholds that lead to the next tier so that it is a comfortable stretch, it is possible to successfully increase your share of a particular customer's business.

  This is where your customer insights can be applied to dangle just the right carrot for them to chase. We know, for example, what a strong incentive being able to use the airport's executive lounge is within an airline loyalty program. Or in a credit card program, charging a minimum amount per year might mean that the next annual fee will be waived.

  Setting the threshold requires some basic data analysis. Look at what the average performer in a segment is doing, and then add a margin that you feel is within reach of a typical customer but which stretches them sufficiently to achieve it. Then, offer an incentive when they get there. It may be that the threshold takes them to a higher tier, or that they receive a gift of some kind. Obviously, if you are offering a gift, the financials must work out such that the profit you make from the incremental business more than pays for the gift. Don't get carried away!

  Making the tiers subject to annual requalification can help to ensure that the customer maintains their new buying habit. You are looking for a program that is going to build your profit base over the long term, not make someone do one thing differently, one time only.

Where a card is being used as the "face" of your CRM program, different cards allow front-line staff to immediately know what benefits or privileges the customer is entitled to.

It is important that you think about the day-to-day application of your CRM program. It must be possible for staff interacting with customers to understand the program, what benefits different customers are entitled to, and how they gain access to them. Aligning groups of benefits to a particular color card is a common and practical way for a customer to demonstrate entitlement, and for the staff member to know what benefits to give.

When to tier

It is not necessary to create a multi-tiered model at the initial launch of your CRM program. Indeed, unless you are in the very fortunate position of having a bulk of quality historical information, it is unlikely that you will be able to determine up-front how many tiers you might need. For example, you may conceive of a program with an entry level and one higher level—let's call them standard and gold. You run the program for 12 months, gather data on customer spending habits, and then analyze what you have.

Think back to the 80:20 rule and ask the following questions:

1. Does the current gold threshold mean that the top 20% of your customers are obtaining a gold card and the services and benefits associated with it? If not, you may need to adjust the entry threshold to the gold tier downward.

2. Do more than the top 20% of your customers benefit? If so, you may have to move the threshold upward.

3. Within your gold group, is there a clear group of very high-value customers that perhaps could be candidates for a platinum card? This may be the top 3–5% by value. If so, does the revenue and profit they bring to you warrant creating an exclusive set of benefits and a card just for them? The answer to this is very likely to be "yes."

If you do elect to launch new tiers later in the program's life, this gives you some real strategic benefits. First, it gives you the advantage of keeping the program alive and growing by injecting new impetus for your current gold card customers—giving them a new motivation, if you like. Second, it will keep your competitors wondering what you are going to launch next. A Chairman's Club, perhaps?

The "Chairman's Club" concept can be applied in many ways. We have used it where you can identify a group of individuals who are very important to you in terms of their personal business, or who are heads of large corporations, and therefore highly influential in terms of the business you might receive, or who are high-profile political figures or celebrities with whom you would like your business to be associated. Entry to the Chairman's Club is normally by invitation by the chairman, and numbers are strictly limited to maintain exclusivity. Frequently, entry is not on the basis of personal performance, although extremely high-value customers may well be invited to join.

To sum up, it is vital to get to grips with the profitability of your customers, because it is the profitable customers who really drive your brand and your business. They have to be looked after to ensure brand loyalty, and other customers, wherever possible, have to be encouraged to aspire to become one of your more profitable customers. Value, frequency, and recency are important metrics to look at when deciding who are your profitable customers, and tiering is an important way of building the profitability concept into a CRM program. At the end of the day, all companies are interested in maximizing the lifetime value of customers—this is the heart of any CRM brand-building program.

6

Implementation Strategy

WHAT ARE THE KEY COMPONENTS TO ESTABLISH YOUR CRM PROGRAM?

Many companies are very keen to embark on a CRM program, but find it difficult to decide where they should start. We suggest that a good place to start is to perform a health check of your company in a number of the key areas, to see how good a shape your company and your brand are in. Undertaking this health check will give you an idea of how much work you will ultimately have to do, and that translates into *how much* your implementation project might cost and *how long* it will take to install. There are six steps involved in this corporate health check, which can lead you to CRM heaven.

SIX STEPS TO CRM HEAVEN

There are six main steps for you to progress through in developing your CRM program. These are:

1. Auditing your systems.
2. Auditing your data.
3. Auditing your existing customer relationships.
4. Auditing your financials.
5. Creating your CRM strategy in line with your brand.
6. Creating your tactical CRM initiatives.

Step 1: Auditing your systems

The current situation

The very first thing to do is to identify each and every "system" that is capturing, manipulating, or holding any piece of data relating to a customer. "System," in this instance, can mean mainframe system, local network, stand-alone PC, Internet site, mobile phone, call center, telephone messaging system, and paper process/storage. It means looking at your sales systems, marketing systems, accounting systems, claims systems, complaints systems, after-sales systems, ticketing/booking systems, credit control systems—that is, every single type of system you have running, past or present, in your company that is likely to have captured, and held, customer data.

You will probably be amazed at what will turn up. Individual marketing departments may have undertaken promotions, with vouchers piled up in the corner of a room or lying forgotten in a drawer. The amount of valuable information that sits around doing nothing in major organizations is criminal. We have seen instances where marketing departments, with good intentions, have run promotions with response slips which customers have completed and returned. Those slips of paper have then sat in a box going to waste, because no one had the manpower available to key them into the marketing system. When you plan your campaigns, think about what needs to happen at the other end. Project the number of responses you are likely to get, and then make sure you have sufficient bodies there to get the data into your system as quickly as possible. We will discuss this in a moment, but most customer data has a useful "sell by" date, and if you don't use it while it is fresh, it quickly becomes useless. People's lives move on, much as you would like to think people are still the same as they were when they filled in your questionnaire. But if you have recent data, there is little point in yet again designing your program and trying to think of the best incentive to get customers to respond. If they have already done so, it is time to use the output.

Looking ahead

You will need to talk to your systems people to find out how readily your systems are capable of handling your proposed program. You need to look at this from a number of angles:

- How easy is it going to be to add additional fields to screen systems for data capture and to your databases for storage?
- How can you link together all the data across your transactional systems to create a customer record? What common data items (or keys) do you have across systems—for example, "name," "date of birth," "identity card number," and "passport number"?
- How can you de-duplicate the data you have across your systems, and how much effort will be involved?
- How quickly can a system be built or sourced to analyze customer data on an ongoing basis, and to use that data to drive customer-specific messages and pricing initiatives?
- How much is it likely to cost, and how long is it likely to take?

All the costs identified during this stage will need to be fed into your project cost/benefit analysis.

Step 2: Auditing your data

Having identified all of the systems capturing and holding customer data, you need to take a closer look at that data. Start by building a list of the customer data items captured by each system. Your listing should note the following:

- What format each data item is in—that is, whether it is text, a number, a percentage, and so on.
- What validation applies to the field when it is captured? Is it compulsory, and therefore you know you have it for every customer? Is the field in a free format, so that anything could be input to it, or are there a limited number of acceptable values (in which case, you will have much more usable data)?

   In the past, systems were usually designed to meet the needs of the exact time they were designed. There was very little forward planning. When old clerical procedures were first mechanized, it was very difficult for marketers to persuade the people who had to do the inputting that there was value in keying in items that were not of immediate use, "just in case we need it later." What it means in practice is that, when you go to these systems now and try to use the data in them, there are often a lot of holes because fields weren't mandatory; the attitude was "We'll key it if we have time." Unfortunately, this means you have more work to do now, before you can move ahead.

- How old the data is—that is, how often it was updated. It is great to have data, but, as mentioned, it is only really useful to you if it is fresh—and the fresher the better. So, establish when the data was last updated.

- Look at the data across the different systems. Are there any items duplicated? If so, which is the more recent/most reliable? You will need to undertake a data merging and de-duplication exercise. Just make sure you remove the older data!

Step 3: Auditing your existing customer relationships

If your program is going to be really successful and give you long-term financial and competitive advantages, you *must* involve your customers in the design process. There is absolutely no point in wasting time and money designing a great marketing program that aims to sell customers everything they could ever ask for or need, if, in their minds, your company specializes in one product and is only ever capable of selling that product. You have to understand how far your brand is capable of being stretched in consumers' minds, and, based on that and your current service delivery, establish the answer to the key question, "Where will your customers give you *permission* to go?" This is important, because, to grow your brand, you will need to extend it to more related, or even unrelated, areas. This ability to extend the brand is often called brand stretch, elasticity, or extension.

Brand stretch (or elasticity)

Staying with one brand offering doesn't offer huge possibilities for growth, but if you want to stretch your brand, there are several things that must be considered here. First there is the fact that if you have a corporate brand, it will be capable of being stretched much more than a single product brand. If we take a product brand like Head and Shoulders shampoo, we can quickly see that the brand wouldn't stand a very good chance of being stretched to cover totally new categories of products, such as consumer electronics or banking. It is only really capable of being extended into different types of shampoo. On the other hand, the corporate brand Virgin, made famous by its founder Richard Branson, has been stretched so far that it covers air travel, financial services, cosmetics, bridal wear, rail travel, vodka, property management, entertainment, publishing, mobile phone operations, and many other activities. Not all the extensions have been phenomenally successful, but they have survived and in many cases are profitable. What makes the Virgin brand so elastic is the single-minded focus on a consistent brand personality, one that customers have a strong emotional association with. (We will discuss brand personality later in this chapter.) Additionally, Virgin management is careful to maintain consistency in its targeting of consumers, only offering its various products and services to the same profile base.

People often ask when a brand can be extended or stretched, and whether there are any rules for this. In fact, there are no right answers to the brand extension question, and to a large extent it is situational. There are some obvious problem areas to watch out for, such as the difficulty in stretching your brand into the premium, luxury area when you are currently in the mainstream, functional type of category. But we can say that with well-managed corporate brands, there is wider scope for offering more products and services than with well-managed product brands, and therefore more scope for employing a CRM program that can cover all customers and the products you offer them, thus leveraging on the elasticity of the brand. So, growing your corporate brand gives you more scope to operate your CRM program.

We mentioned the word "permission" above. This is a key word, because if you start trying to sell your customer base items under your brand that they don't believe you have the knowledge or expertise to produce, or if they don't perceive the new offering to fit with what the brand stands for, then they won't buy. Similarly, if your customer base lacks a strong emotional association with your brand, then it will be more difficult for you to stretch it. And no matter how much marketing material you bombard them with, you won't change their minds. What you need to do is to find out where you currently have permission to tread, and the answer lies in research within your customer base. We have touched on this subject in the preceding chapters, but there is *absolutely no substitute for talking to your customers*, and you need to work out the most effective means for doing this.

Here are some ideas on the kind of information needed as background to the development of a CRM program.

Qualitative versus quantitative research

For those of you who are not conversant with research terminology, *quantitative research* tends to be shallower in terms of the amount of questioning, but is conducted over a much larger number of people. Quantitative research usually determines what is happening in a market, and might be used, for example, to determine the size and make-up of a particular market segment, which brands they buy, where they buy them from, when, and so on. It tends to be questionnaire-based, using large samples from door-to-door or street surveys, the telephone, or the Internet.

Qualitative research is concerned more with observing what happens and explaining why it happens. It is very useful for testing how consumers feel about things such as the brand personality, the brand experience, and new initiatives, like those contained in a CRM program. Qualitative research is in-depth research among a relatively small number of people, and would normally take the form of individual, in-depth, face-to-face interviews, or focus groups of between eight and 12 people (or perhaps mini-groups of five to eight people).

There are arguments for using each technique, and indeed a combination of the two, and we have found that the best results occur when both are used. Here are a couple of examples of how the techniques can be used together.

Quantitative leading, qualitative following. Working in Asia with Malaysia Airlines, we needed to understand what their passengers felt about the service they currently delivered, what their expectations of them were as a national carrier, and how the airline could build real added value into its Enrich frequent flyer program.

The approach we took was first to hand out questionnaires on the aircraft on selected sectors to try and get a better understanding of who was using the airline and why they used it. We asked them to score the airline on a number of key service factors pre-flight, during flight, and post-flight. We then proposed a number of potential added-value benefits the airline might be able to give to them and asked for their views. The final question on the questionnaire was to find out whether they would be prepared to participate in further research if asked. By including this question, we were able to put together a pool of people that we could use to draw our focus groups from.

The questionnaire was incredibly effective—the majority we had returned were fully completed, and, as we often find, a number of customers had inserted extra sheets of paper and gone into some detail about what they would like to see happen.

From our pool of ready and willing respondents, we then went on to run focus groups of from eight to 10 people. We divided our target groups between heavy users of first and business class, and heavy economy users. We carried out in-depth discussions within the groups to probe into the data we had pulled together from the questionnaire. This allowed us to put together a first cut of the CRM program we needed to put in place.

This approach seems to work well, in our experience. We have used it with insurance companies, major cinema chains, within the car distribution sector, and even with a symphony hall!

Spend time getting the questionnaire right in the first place. You will find you will get a much higher response rate if you make it visually interesting. Don't just hand out a plain sheet with tick boxes. Make it colorful, make it fun, and pre-fill anything that you can, to make life easier for the recipient. Include a return envelope and probably some form of incentive. We have used vouchers, mystery gifts, and cash prize draws. You will need to decide what is appropriate for your business and your situation.

Qualitative leading, quantitative following. Working on a project with a large telecommunications company, we needed to find out quickly what customers really felt about their service and what the likelihood was of customers defecting to a new provider when the Singaporean telecommunications market deregulated.

We approached this by first interviewing a number of their long-term customers, focusing on the higher-value groups, but also involving some who were lower down the value range. By talking to them, we were quickly able to build a picture of the questions we needed to ask the wider customer base. We then developed a questionnaire that was mailed out to around 12,000 people.

We approached it in this way because we felt we needed to test our own understanding of the key issues we wanted the wider group to comment on. We had been able to put together our first thoughts from the interviews we carried out within the client's organization. Their own research team had a good deal of information already, but it can be dangerous to assume too much. It always pays to ask the customers directly, rather than rely on third-hand information.

You need to decide which approach is most suited to your own circumstances, and to take advice if you are not sure. How confident do you feel about the key questions you need answers to in order to be able to construct your questionnaire?

What information are you trying to find?

We would like to cover some areas of qualitative information that are useful for focusing on prior to implementing a CRM program. These are all to do with finding out what consumers feel about your brand, because it is the emotional side of consumer behavior that drives people to and away from brands. Basically, consumers are thinking several things about your brand when they are deciding whether or not to buy it or to opt for another. Some of the more important of these thoughts are:

- Are you efficient and effective at what you do and offer?
- Can you give me things that I really value, and not just the basics?
- Can you *not* give me the things I don't value?
- Do you know the things you do that annoy me, and are you willing to change your behavior?

- Can you demonstrate to me why your brand is different and better than the others?

Every company has to get to grips with these questions, and that means, first of all, getting the information from the consumer that will help you to deal with them. You might ask them, for example:

- What are the things they particularly *like* about your product, your service, or the brand values? Do they understand what the brand stands for?
- What are the things they *dislike* about your brand? What have you done to upset them? What are their "pet hates" about the way you do business?
- If they could change three things about your brand, what would they be?
- Who do they see as your key competitors? What are their relative good points and bad points? How are they different from and better than your brand? How do their brand values compare to yours?
- How likely are they to keep doing business with you if your brand doesn't change?
- If your brand was to improve in their identified key areas, how likely are they to do more business with you?
- How much do they currently spend with you per month/year?
- How much do they spend with your key competitors per month/year?

All this information will give you fundamentally important data with which to work out the financial case for your program, but it will do much more than this—it will help you to understand the answer to the key issues of how you can strengthen your existing brand, and where your customers will allow you to go with it. It will be a foundation stone for your CRM program.

Step 4: Auditing your financials

Whether you like it or not, the ultimate answer to the question, "Was the project a success?" will be a judgment made against your projected financials. You will need to construct a financial case for your CRM project which looks at what the current situation is, and what you think you can move it to.

Before you can construct that financial model, you will need to understand some of the key financial drivers of your business, such as:

- How much it costs currently to obtain a new customer.
- How much you currently have to spend to hold on to that customer each year.
- How much profit each customer will make for you if you manage to continue to do business with them over an extended period of time.

You then need to begin to look at how much extra profit you could be making by changing the habits of the customer. We will go into this in some detail toward the end of this chapter.

The best way to approach the financial analysis is to work very closely with your finance division to construct the model. In fact, the most powerful approach is to get them to build the model for you. That way, there can be no arguments between marketing and finance about whether or not the numbers are correct. It is also very powerful when the finance team makes the report on your project to your board or CEO. If *you* present the numbers, they will be asked to verify them in any event. So, make life easy for yourself. If your finance director isn't your best friend currently, get to work!

Step 5: Creating your CRM strategy in line with your brand

Once you have all the information you need to hand, you can begin to construct your CRM strategy—the customer relationship blueprint, which consists of the components shown in Figure 6.1.

The customer relationship blueprint is merely a structured approach to defining and installing your CRM program. It is an attempt to break down a significant piece of foundational work into manageable chunks of effort.

Organizations cannot change overnight, so you need to scope out a number of key initiatives you can take to move you toward your desired

Figure 6.1: The customer relationship blueprint

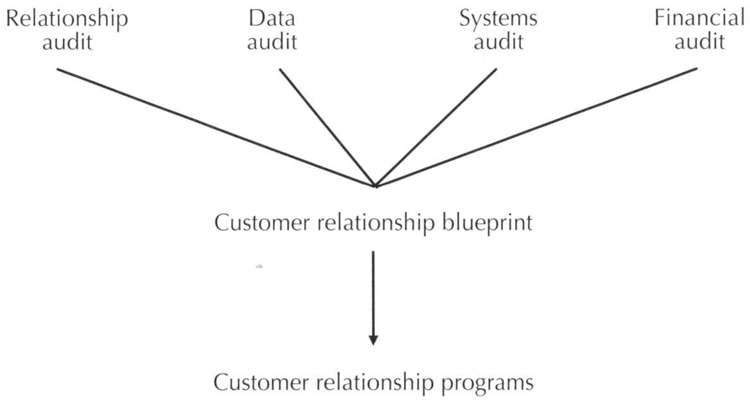

state. Remember that old project management saying: "How do you eat an elephant? One bite at a time." This is the secret to your success. There is no need to do everything in one go; just build one component at a time. Each initiative you get up-and-running will have an immediate positive impact on the business.

Also, it is not necessary to have the same people undertake each of the chunks. In practice, you are likely to have people who are skilled in each of the areas who can get the information you need, and then you can oversee the entire operation.

Key components of CRM strategy

In creating your CRM strategy, it is important that you cover the following areas:

- Make your company the type of company people really want to do business with over and over again (through reskilling, restructuring, and retooling).
- Create a mechanism to identify, reward, and therefore retain your best customers (through customer reward and recognition programs).
- Create a means to organically grow the value of your existing customer base (through cross-selling and up-selling).
- Find new customers with the right potential (through "member get member" activities).

But before we pay attention to these issues, one of the most important things to do is to make sure that the CRM strategy is aligned to the company's brand strategy.

Let brand strategy drive CRM strategy in the softer issues

You need a strategy to take you from the type of organization you are today, to the type of organization your customers are telling you they would most like you to be. Essentially, it is an organizational change program, but not a superficial one. Instead, it should be one that gets into the heart of the company and changes it to become the customers' trusted friend. To do that, you must concentrate on developing your brand to its fullest potential, and for this you need a brand strategy. A brand strategy relies on two main elements:

- a likeable brand personality; and
- a strong positioning strategy.

Brand personality. Brands, as described in Chapter 1, are the very heart of a good consumer relationship. Brands have emotional impact on consumers, and the greater that emotional impact is, the greater their loyalty will be to your company. In building brands, companies use the concept of a "brand personality" to bring out the emotion in people they want to attract and keep.

The "personality" of a company or its brand is a very important factor in any CRM initiative. The world's greatest brands consciously build personalities for their corporate and product brands. They do this because consumers readily relate to people, and tend to judge a company's performance in personality terms. For example, two women were heard talking as they left a retail outlet that sold watches and writing instruments. One said to the other, "I'm not going in there again; the people are so unfriendly." The brand experience they had received was so bad that the shop had clearly lost two customers, and maybe more after they had told their friends.

CRM is all about giving the consumer a great brand experience, and to do this every company has to decide what that experience is going to be like. It isn't good enough, for example, to write to valued customers and start by saying "Dear Valued Customer," because their reaction is going to be: "If I'm so valued, how come the company doesn't address me by name?" Little things like this mean a lot. The company may think it is being "friendly and caring," but the experience suggests otherwise.

It will help you to relate to consumers if you think of your organization as a person. One exercise we do with management teams is to get them to answer the following two questions:

• If you were to describe your company now as a person, what words would you use?

• If you were to describe your company in terms of what kind of person you would like it to be in the future, what words would you use?

The more people in your organization you ask these questions of, the clearer idea you will get of the current truth about the brand and their aspirations for it. Examples of positive words that people think of might be *reliable, confident, friendly, sophisticated, trustworthy, caring, innovative, knowledgeable, professional*, and so on. Negative words might include *bureaucratic, inflexible, unfriendly*, and *not creative*.

After going through this process internally, it is then worth asking customers these questions as well, because you will gain a quick and important insight into the brand personality as they perceive it. People think in people terms, and can easily use personality characteristics to describe companies and their relationships with them. So, get some customers of your company, and customers of other companies if you can, and ask them the same two questions. Spend as much time as you need looking through your customer responses, to really understand what they want from you. What are they saying about you? You might find comments about being *remote* or *unresponsive*, or *inflexible*, or perhaps *poor at communicating, arrogant*, or *self-centered*. Do any of these words describe your company? Also look out for positive things customers are saying about you, because you need to make more of these brand strengths. Examples might be *good at listening, helpful, caring, responsive, flexible*, and *approachable*.

When you are making a final selection of personality characteristics for your brand, make sure you have a good balance of rational and emotional attributes. For example, you might think that for your business, you need a brand that projects a personality that is reliable, efficient, and fast. This is fine, but it is a cold type of personality—there isn't much warmth there. What it needs is a couple more attributes that will bring emotions into play, such as responsive, friendly, warm, or approachable. The exact combination of attributes depends on each company and its situation, and also on what consumers and staff want to experience and be. Paul Temporal's book *Branding in Asia* (Published by John Wiley & Sons, 2000) contains in-depth analysis and examples of how to build a powerful brand through this methodology.

When you have the results of this brand personality analysis, you will then have to conceive the initiatives—the individual projects—that will change the way the customer sees you, as shown in Figure 6.2. We will illustrate how these might be accomplished shortly.

Brand personality consistency. The brand personality that you have established in the questioning process above needs to be applied consistently to every part of the company's business, especially where the company has contact with the customer, as with CRM and customer service programs. It is also important for back-room operations to adopt the same personality, as their work will affect the customers' brand

Figure 6.2: Moving toward your desired state

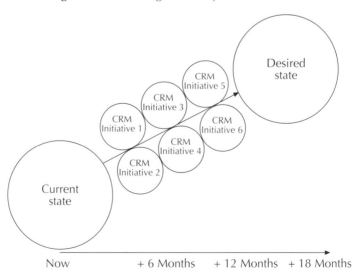

experience. If you consistently project and action this personality, and if it is one that consumers like, then it will attract and retain them. They will become friends with your brand and, like friends, they will be loyal.

Brand positioning. When you have successfully created the brand personality that will be the outward face of your CRM program, you need to think about a positioning strategy that will answer the two questions that consumers have uppermost in their minds, namely:

- Why are you different?
- Why are you better?

In order to answer these questions, you will have to take a good look at what your competitors are doing.

What are your competitors up to?

As well as all the data you have gathered so far, you will need to look at your competitive backdrop. Do any of your competitors currently have CRM or loyalty programs running? If they do, you need to find out as much information about them as you possibly can. This needs to go beyond what is in the public domain, so you will need to get yourself or your colleagues enrolled in as many of their programs as possible. The reason for this is that with good CRM programs, there are frequently things going on which you would never pick up on unless you are actively participating in those programs. For example, there may be subtle differences in the detail of the communications, or the way in which promotions are being targeted, or highly personalized touches, such as phone calls from customer managers. All competitor programs ought to be continually monitored. Build something into your marketing budget to enable your peer group to participate at the company's expense. This is invaluable information to have, and it will enable them to see how each competitor is positioning its brand, what personality that brand has, and what you need to do with your brand and CRM program to make them different.

Writing a positioning statement

When you have analyzed the competition and defined your personality, you can then write a positioning statement that will serve as a guide for internal staff and external agencies as to how your brand should be represented in the marketplace. One way of doing this is to follow the template outline below.

OUR BRAND

is better than

(state the names of competing brands)

for

(state the specific target customer groups)

because it has

(state your strategic competitive advantage/s)

with the result that

(state how the consumer benefits)

It is worthwhile spending some time with your team to get this statement right, and to include in its text the personality characteristics of the brand. Several iterations are sometimes required, but the end-product will give everyone clear direction as to what you should be thinking of in generating and implementing your CRM strategy.

Step 6: Creating your tactical CRM initiatives

With your strategy in place, you need to map out the CRM initiatives that you intend to undertake in the next 12 to 18 months to fulfill your strategy.

Scoping out the CRM initiatives

We need to return to our diagram (see Figure 6.3) to illustrate how you can mobilize the knowledge you now have, via specific CRM initiatives—initiatives that will turn you from the kind of company your customers are saying you are now, into the kind of company they are saying they would like you to be. Remember that, whether or not you agree with what they are saying, it is their perception, and that is all that counts. It is changing their perception that is critical and that will have the biggest impact on your business.

Start by putting together, from your research, a statement of how your customers view you currently. For this illustration, we have assumed that the labels *inflexible*, *difficult to access*, *not customer-focused*, *slow to respond*, *unreliable*, *cheap*, and *low quality* have been distilled out as key areas for the strategic improvement of the brand, and that CRM is to be the thrust for this.

Now, how would consumers *like* to see you? What would you like your brand to be seen as? It is likely to be the opposite of many of the labels you have used—for example, your desired state could well be to be

Figure 6.3: Applying your new knowledge

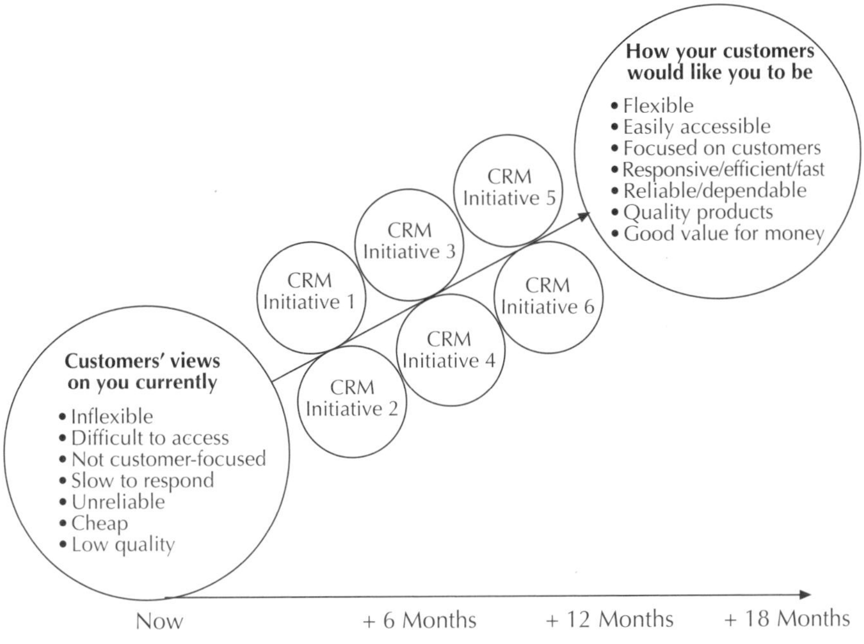

thought of as *flexible, easily accessible, focused on customers, responsive/ efficient/fast*, and *reliable/dependable*. You may also want to use your CRM initiatives to try and take your brand a little more upmarket—to be regarded as offering quality products that are not necessarily cheap but perhaps good value for money.

When you have deliberated on this, and know where you want to get to, the next question is: How can you get there? Based on these examples, we will address each point separately in order to give some ideas as to how CRM can help the brand-building process.

From "inflexible" to "flexible." Often, a perception of being inflexible comes from front-line staff not being empowered to make decisions that affect the customer. Where an organization has a massive rules book or handbook that staff must comply with, front-line staff often become frustrated, and customers more so.

In retailing, for instance, many of the decisions that front-line employees currently refer to a floor supervisor could be delegated to front-liners. For example, if a customer brings something back for a refund and this currently requires a supervisor's signature for a refund to be given, is it *really* necessary? If there is opposition to front-liners having open-ended authority, they could be given a limit that they can work within—say, $100. There is nothing more frustrating to a customer than a front-liner saying, "Can you wait while I get my supervisor?", especially when the store is busy and there are many demands on the supervisor. If staff members have the authority to sell, shouldn't they also have the authority to refund? Not all customers feel comfortable about returning goods. It can be stressful, so make the experience as free of fuss as possible. Marks and Spencer is renowned for its returns policy, where refunds are given immediately and without question.

A CRM initiative coming out of this could be: "To review decision points and look at greater staff empowerment." Supplementary to this may be a number of systems or process initiatives. If you push decision making closer to the front line, you may well need to extend your management information systems to audit activities. You may also need to run a number of training sessions to help your front-line staff and make them feel comfortable with their new powers.

Let's return briefly to the first point of customer intimacy for a moment. One of the keys to the success of your CRM initiative will be creating a mechanism that allows you to become intimate with the customer. You have to bring it down to 1:1 (see Figure 6.4), because no matter how big your organization is, or how many customers you have, at some point there will be one individual from your company interacting with one of your customers. We want to emphasize this point because it is such a key theme of this book. You have to be brave enough to push as much decision making as possible to that point of interaction between your brand and the consumer. Consequently, you have to give your representatives as wide a skills base as possible.

Try to think of your staff member as the owner of the Mom and Pop store we referred to at the beginning of the book. What would they need to know, and what decisions must they be able to take each day? Remember, as far as your customers are concerned, each member of your staff *is* the company. You have given them the responsibility of representing your company and your brand each and every day. You must give them the skills and the authority to be able to do that job to the very best of their ability, and give every single customer the very best brand experience.

From "difficult to access" to "easily accessible." Large organizations can be notoriously difficult to communicate with. How many times have you rung the switchboard of a corporation, and then been passed from pillar to post, trying to find the right person to talk to, to get your problem resolved? Worse still are some of the telephone schemes meant to be part of CRM initiatives, which have customers pressing button

Figure 6.4: The point of interaction

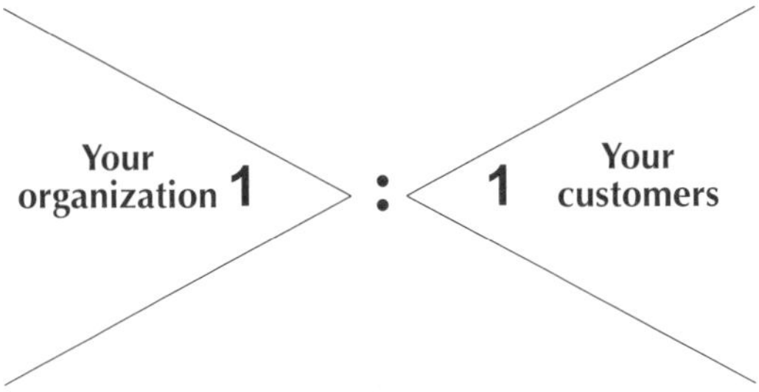

after button to eventually get to, "We're sorry, all our assistants are engaged at the moment. Your call is important to us. Please hold."

What CRM initiative could resolve this type of situation? You would need to think in terms of creating a single customer service team with the authority to resolve issues from any division within the organization. This team would provide a single point of contact into your company, and team members would take immediate ownership of problems, complaints, requests for information, accounts queries—any type of possible communication from a customer to your company.

One of the ways to help create such a team is to develop "short fat people", as opposed to "tall thin people." This isn't a provocative health imperative, but a good CRM culture builder. What we mean by this is simply that within most major organizations, people tend to enter one particular line or division and develop their skills within that division. As the careers of employees progress, they become more and more technically competent within their chosen area, whether it is accounts, sales, marketing, or whatever. They tend to become "tall thin people" who know a lot about one particular area of the business. These people may be of great benefit in the back office, but they will find it difficult in the front office, where they will encounter a range of different problems from customers. What are needed are "short fat people"—people who are multiskilled, and who have a good understanding across all the key areas of the business. They don't have to know all the technical "ins and outs," as your "tall thin people" are there to provide that support. But they need to know enough to be able to answer the majority of questions customers put to them without the need to refer upwards.

So, what is required is to understand the typical questions coming into your company. Select a team of people, give them the necessary skills training, and then give them the systems and support they need to be able to deliver an excellent first response to your customers. Once they are in place, proactively communicate the fact to your customers, and give a direct dial number so that they no longer need to go through your switchboard.

If you don't feel you have the ability to achieve this internally, an alternative is to employ an external call center to fulfill this role. We have used this route to great effect on a number of occasions. We always say that, for this particular purpose, it is better to find people who enjoy dealing with customers and give them the technical skills, rather than try to give technical people customer skills. The latter solution doesn't tend to work well.

Call centers tend to recruit people with the required sorts of skills, and with the correct training and systems support it doesn't take long to get them up and running. We have heard all sorts of reasons as to why you should use technically trained people—most often, "Because it takes years to train a person to be able to do this." In our experience, good people can learn most of what they need in an intensive six- to eight-week training period.

From "not customer-focused" to "customer-focused." We have already talked at some length about restructuring your organization to make it customer-centric, and you will need to review your current structure and the roles within it. Relevant questions include: Does your company only have product managers and brand managers, or do you have customer managers in place? Can you remove any layers within your structure? (Having customer managers and flatter structures means that more people are closer to the customer.)

Your newly formed "first point of contact" team will certainly help to demonstrate a degree of customer focus. Putting the customer first requires a change of mindsets, so you should consider a training initiative to get across to your staff how important *thinking of the customer* is to your company's well-being. Reinforce the fact to your staff that it is the customer who puts the money in their pay packet each month.

From "slow to respond" to "responsive/efficient/fast." Lack of response to customers can result from a number of things:

- It may be that there are too many steps, or too many people, involved in the process. We mentioned earlier the desirability of re-engineering your processes back from the customer and removing any redundant steps. If processes can be shortened, this will mean increased responsiveness.

- It may be that you are dependent on third-party suppliers to respond, and that you need to review your contractual agreements with them. Do you have service levels built into your agreements? It is fashionable to use "just in time" (JIT) ordering to keep stock costs down. If your company uses this method, ensure that the process works and that you are not left without stock and with disappointed customers.

- Lack of customer information at the point of interaction with the customer can mean that immediate action isn't possible. Review your support systems, and make as much information about the customer as possible available at the point of sale/service.

- Are you still running a 9 to 5 operation? If you are servicing customers, 9 to 5 doesn't cut it anymore. Most people these days work extended hours, and have very little time during the day to undertake activities such as banking or shopping. Customers often try to contact organizations after 5 p.m., and if they are met with an answer phone service they are quite likely to feel neglected when they need you. If you cannot get your current staff to work longer hours or shift patterns, change your staff, or consider outsourcing your customer contact after "normal" hours.

Here is an example of how one company became much faster in responding to customer orders.

Case Study 10
EXABYTE CORPORATION
Faster response to customer orders

The world's largest manufacturer and distributor of tape backup and intelligent, automated data storage solutions also has an integrated CRM technology system. With this addition, Exabyte can receive customer orders from anywhere in the world and ship products from any location, slashing its order fulfillment time from 14 days to one day. Ties among the financial, order entry, scheduling, inventory, and asset management applications provide an immediate view of and reporting on overseas inventory, back stocks, sales, order status, and cost performance. The online workflow, involving more than 900 Oracle users, improves operational efficiencies and increases transaction processing. In addition, through the financial applications, Exabyte is able to view immediate versus monthly analysis.

Source: Oracle Corporation

From "unreliable" to "reliable/dependable." Perceived unreliability can be the result of staff merely failing to keep promises made to customers. Alternatively, it can occur because there are not enough checks in place within the organizational systems to ensure that products have been delivered or orders placed, or work has been completed on time. However, the fact remains that unreliability of any sort can kill a good brand.

In the case of the former, this is an important area to pick up on in your "customer first" training. All of us have been guilty at some point of not fulfilling a promise, but if you tell someone you are going to do something, you should do it—especially if it is a paying customer. We understand that sometimes technology and suppliers conspire against you, but being reliable is a mindset that must be adopted by your organization. "Promises to customers are sacred." We recall this mantra from a "customer care" workshop held at a client's office in the U.K. They ended up with a reminder pinned on the wall of their office: "Have you delivered the milk today?" (Many English homes still have milk delivered to their door first thing each day, come rain or snow.) Find a phrase that suits your organization, but deliver those promises every day.

Check the information available to you from within your systems so that you can track the progress of orders, jobs, claims, account payments—whatever is the particular product or service you are responsible for. A good tracking system shouldn't require you to wade through pages of reports trying to see anything that is abnormal. Build a system process to do that for you. All you want is an exception report, on screen or paper, listing those cases where you are failing to deliver on your promises. Systems should make it easier to manage your workload, not create more work for you.

From "low-quality products" to "quality products." This is a critical item, because you will never be able to build a strong brand without a good-quality product or service. There is little in the way of advice we can give here, except to adopt the highest possible quality standards you can in every possible encounter with the consumer. We do suggest, however, that you benchmark your brand against the competition (and other strong brands outside your category or industry) to get a view of how you are perceived by consumers as far as quality is concerned. If your image is one of poor quality, it may take years to change deeply entrenched perceptions about quality. If you are doing well, there will still be some improvements to make. The search for best quality is a never-ending one.

From "cheap" to "value for money." The value for money (VFM) position is a great one for a company to have, but it is as well to remember that value isn't just about price. In fact, research tells us that, in any industry, price is only a deciding factor when everything else is equal. Brands that have the "cheap" tag are usually those that spend all their time discounting and offering constant sales and promotions, so try to avoid these. Competing on price is a death strategy unless you can always be the industry cost leader. Even if this is achieved—which is no mean feat—margins will inevitably be low and the name of the game will be chasing volume. So, it is best to avoid the commodity trap, and you can do this effectively by constantly looking at ways in which value can be added to the brand. This is where CRM comes in, because it has the potential, as we have described, to bring many benefits to the consumer that all help to build the perception of great brand value.

Tesco is a very good example of a brand that managed to take itself out of a middle-to-downmarket position to become the top food retailer in Europe. It all started with the Clubcard initiative and the change of attitude within the store, which led to an increased focus on the customer and customer service. Case Study 11, toward the end of this chapter, explains how Tesco transformed its brand and shifted to a high-value, high-quality proposition.

If we return to our diagram and put in our CRM initiatives (see Figure 6.5), you should get a better feel for how to move ahead yourself.

Figure 6.5: CRM initiatives scoped out and in place.

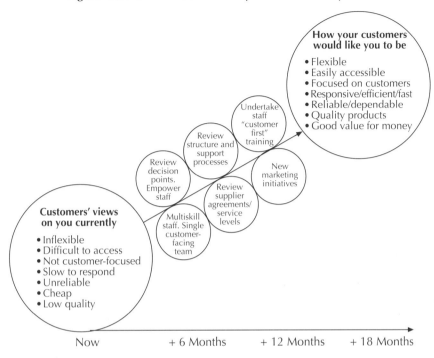

We have described the following CRM initiatives, which are in no particular order. You can define a particular order based on the strength of feeling for each problem area within your research.

1. Review decision points. Empower staff.
2. Multiskill staff. Single customer-facing team.
3. Review structure and support processes.
4. Review supplier agreements and service levels.
5. Undertake staff "customer first" training.
6. New marketing initiatives.

Each of these initiatives will need to be scoped out in more detail, but we hope this gives you an idea of how to approach your own CRM project. Notice that of the six initiatives, only one is directly under the marketing function. Most of them are under customer services, human resources, and finance/purchasing. This means that the whole organization must work together to achieve the same end, and that the project must be owned at the highest level possible.

CHECKLIST FOR NEW CRM MARKETING INITIATIVES

Let's take time out to review, in the form of a brief checklist, what is required to make up new CRM marketing initiatives.

1. Build up your segmentation profile of your customer base and establish who your highest-value customers are.

2. Think about whether or not you want to install a reward program. If you do, what form should it take? Is it a "spend money and earn/ redeem points for prizes" approach? Do you feel that it might be more appropriate to create a recognition program, one that offers exclusive privileges for your best customers?

3. Look at what your customers are buying from you. How can you encourage them to buy more from you? Can you give them an additional service to try for free for a month, and then a discount if they go on to buy it from you? If someone regularly buys one product from you, can you sell them a different product? Find out what they need and what you could sell them.

4. Put your "member get member" program together. Ask your current customers to introduce you to a family member, or a friend or colleague. Offer them a reward for doing so—we guarantee that with your new responsive customer-focused business, your "member get member" campaign will be highly successful for you. You will get much better results than with other forms of promotion, and if you focus on your higher-value customers, you will tend to attract good-quality leads. Try it once and see if you don't agree.

5. The final reality check. You have your master plan in place, but before you rush headlong into kicking off all the project work, if you have the budget and the time, we would strongly recommend that you go back to your original focus groups and get their opinions on what you are proposing. Does it make sense to them? And, importantly, do they feel it would influence the way they are likely

to behave? After all, the ultimate test is whether they are likely to do more business with you if you are able to make your plan a reality.

THE CASE FOR EXTERNAL ASSISTANCE

If you are pioneering the CRM thinking within your organization, you may have to undertake a good degree of the initial work yourself before additional internal resources will be made available to you. In these circumstances, it is well worth considering enlisting the help of a marketing agency to help you put a high-level cost case together. It may well also be the case that, at least during the running of the pilot project, it makes more sense to use agency resources than to permanently increase the size of your establishment.

If you pick your agency with care, you should find that they have been through the pain of these projects before and can guide you away from all the "danger zones"—the things that are likely to slow you down or even bring your project to a complete halt. Such problems tend to be political in nature and can be minimized by obtaining buy-in to the program at the highest level. For instance, the CEO needs to understand the principle and what it is going to do for the company. An external agency may be able to help you sell CRM and its benefits to your CEO.

The other big benefit of using an agency, assuming you pick one that has experience in launching and running CRM programs, is that they will have systems and people in place ready and waiting. You won't need to build systems from scratch, as they are likely to be able to clone something that they have used before for your pilot. It really is a fast track to getting out there.

Face the fact that if you are thinking about the merits of CRM, there is a pretty good chance your competitors are doing so too. There are no prizes for being second in this game, so any chance to get into the market sooner than the competition should be seized.

When we first started working with CRM techniques, there were probably only a handful of companies worldwide who both understood the concepts and had experience of applying them in practice. Today, thankfully, there are many agencies that have been successful in practicing the techniques, and you should not have too much trouble in finding the right one for you.

Selecting an agency to help you

There are a number of sensible approaches you can take to selecting which marketing agency you will ultimately work with. When you think about the amount of money likely to be paid out, you should ensure that it is going to be money well spent.

The reality is that in a typical organization, there are likely to have been a handful of people who have had first-hand experience of appointing an agency. It may well be that such an appointment needs to be made by the board, but this isn't typical. Something as important as appointing your corporate advertising agency is likely to be a board decision, but marketing agencies seem to make their way into an organization at relatively low levels.

As we have already stated, the brand impact of a good CRM program is at least as far-reaching as any advertising campaign you may run. Appointment of the marketing agency should therefore be taken in a similar light. If it becomes your responsibility to appoint the agency and you are uncomfortable about the selection process, seek help from people in your organization who have the relevant experience.

Selection processes

Often, when a company wants to appoint an agency, they will issue invitations to suitable agencies to come in and deliver what is known as a credentials presentation. This normally constitutes the agency presenting their key team members, giving details about the agency's ownership, size, and core competencies, then walking you through examples of their previous work.

Taking references

It is a good idea at this stage to ask if you can speak to or visit a few of the agency's existing clients. This will give you a view of how well the client feels the agency is performing against their expectations. The agency will probably try and arrange a visit and come along with you. Try to resist this, because it is unlikely that you will get an open and honest opinion in the presence of the agency.

As with anything else, you will get more out of the discussions if you prepare for them in advance, so create a list of questions you would like answers to. Probably a good place to start is: Does the client feel they are getting value for money? This is normally a good indicator of the state of the client–agency relationship.

Competitive tender

The next stage is typically to give the short-listed agencies a brief for your project, asking them to present how they would approach it, and to give realistic costs for their projected activity. This is called a pitch, and the successful agency is chosen usually by a panel of company representatives, many of whom will have an interest, operationally or financially, in the program.

When putting your project out to competitive tender, the things you should build into the selection process include:

- **Agency's brand-building experience**: Unfortunately, not all CRM agencies have a good knowledge of what branding is all about, and few will have extensive experience of actually building one. They may be technically very good, but lack brand-building skill. However, it is important that you find one that has brand-building experience, because CRM activities are so high profile that a poorly thought-out and executed program can seriously damage a company's brand image. Also, it is the brand personality and positioning that need to be taken from the brief you give to the agency and turned into the appropriate look and feel, and tone and manner, of your customer communications.

- **Recommendations**: One way around some of the selection problems is to ask anyone who is currently working on a CRM project, or has installed a CRM program, if they can recommend an agency to you.

- **Cultural fit**: At the end of the day, you have to work closely with the people in the agency you select. Ensure that you are clear about who your day-to-day contacts will be, and make sure they are people who you feel comfortable working with. It doesn't matter how good the agency is overall if you don't feel you can work with their people. They have to be people you feel you can build a strong working relationship with and entrust the success of your project to. One final point to watch out for here is that, when pitching for new clients, agencies normally put forward their best people in an effort to impress, but may not use all those people on the project once they have been awarded it. So, before you sign the contract, make sure it contains the names of those people who will be on your project team, and check that they are the ones you want.

The following two case studies illustrate world-class CRM implementation strategies.

Case Study 11
TESCO PLC
Building brand leadership with CRM

Introduction

This case study provides a compelling business model, whether your business is financial services, retailing, or even business-to-business marketing.

Tesco is the leading light in the U.K. grocery retailing market, consistently outperforming its competitors in an increasingly competitive marketplace. But that certainly wasn't the situation a decade ago. Much of Tesco's success since then can be attributed to the launch of Tesco's Clubcard program, which has evolved over that time from a reward program to a CRM program that is so integral to the daily operations of the retailer that, to quote Tim Mason, Tesco's marketing director, "Tesco wouldn't be Tesco now without Clubcard. It is used to run our business. We use it for planning new stores, in new product development, to understand who is buying what products, and in planning our promotions."

Many of the U.K. retailers use loyalty cards, but no one has been able to replicate the phenomenal success of Clubcard. To steal a line from a James Bond film, "Nobody does it better." There are two million Clubcard holders. There are 22 million households in the U.K. The secret to that success, according to Tim Mason, is that Tesco employs teams both inside and outside the company to analyze the card data. The amount of data it now holds on its Clubcard customers means that in a single voucher mail-out there may be as many as 80,000 different permutations. This is mass customization in practice.

Background

Tesco was founded by Sir Jack Cohen with a "pile it high, sell it cheap" philosophy, typical of many supermarkets of the time. For 25 years or more, the U.K. market had been dominated by J. Sainsbury. Other key players in the market over the years have included Gateway, Asda, and Safeway. J. Sainsbury was recognized as the place to go for quality food at reasonable prices, but with high-quality stores and excellent staff and service.

Tesco, even 10 years ago, would have been viewed as a second-league store. Everything was fine, but nothing about it made it a place that everyone headed for—it lacked a strong brand. At that time, it tended to have medium-sized stores on the high street. Over the years, the U.K. has followed the U.S. trend toward bigger, out-of-town stores that offer more choice and facilities for customers. Most people in the U.K. now live within 20 minutes' drive of two or three of the main competitor stores, typically J. Sainsbury, Tesco and one other, depending on the location.

For most people, shopping for food is a chore, and one that we have to undertake more frequently than we might wish. There is therefore a strong natural incentive to use a variety of stores, to relieve the boredom as much as anything else.

The U.K. food retailing market has been mature for years. The U.K. population, generally speaking, already eats too much, so there is no natural growth in the market. Therefore, any growth made by an individual retailer has to be at the expense of market share for its competitors. To increase market share in this stagnant situation, most retailers have increasingly run advertising campaigns coupled with short-term, price-based promotions in an attempt to drive customers into their stores. This type of activity, however, tends to encourage customers to shop around from store to store, which is exactly what the retailers *don't* want to happen.

Tesco looks for something new

In 1992, when an economic recession hit the U.K., all retailers, including Tesco, were hard hit. Tesco tried to advertise its way to more customers, but with little impact. The company then tried something revolutionary. It interviewed 250,000 of its customers *and asked them what they wanted from the store.* Customers gave guidance on specific food lines they wanted, but the overriding message that came back was that customers were looking for better value.

At this time, Tesco appointed a new marketing director, Terry Leahy. Leahy didn't hail from a traditional marketing background, but had worked previously within Tesco as a buyer. He has since become chief executive of Tesco's empire of 750 stores in the U.K. and its rapidly expanding overseas business. So, what did Terry Leahy do at Tesco to take the brand from the middle order to the undisputed leader of the U.K. grocery retailing market? As well as introducing Tesco's own "Value" house brand, he set about making Tesco a better place to shop. He transformed the stores from being cheap and dowdy, to places where middle-class Britons were happy to do their shopping.

Staff were retrained to focus on looking after customers as a priority, rather than stocking the shelves. Tesco created "Customer Assistants" to help customers pack their shopping and carry their bags to their car. They introduced an initiative called "One in front" to try and reduce the queues at checkout counters. It works on the principle that if there is more than one person in the queue in front of a customer, Tesco will open up more tills to the point where every single one is working. This requires staff to be multiskilled, so that they can be called to the tills during busy periods.

The beginnings of Clubcard

On top of all this, Terry Leahy began working on developing a store loyalty card. As a buyer, he couldn't see the sense in the pricing policy being operated within retail stores. As a buyer, he expected to be given better prices if he ordered a large volume of product than if he ordered a small quantity. But pretty much all stores at that time offered the same price and the same service to customers, irrespective of how much they bought or how often they visited.

Leahy began to look for a mechanism to reward customers, based on the amount of money they spent with the store. What he quickly realized was that the key to the growth of the company was to get shoppers to keep returning to Tesco's stores, rather than tackling competitors head-on with pricing and advertising wars. We have heard that he actually sent scouting parties around the world looking for new ideas, and through this he stumbled upon the magnetic stripe card that became the Clubcard.

Introduced in 1994 on a trial basis, the scheme was so successful it was rolled out nationally in February 1995. We still remember the advertising when the card was launched. The key message was, "Tesco just wants to say 'Thank you'." This was unheard of. No retailer had every publicly thanked its customers for their business, and this alone captured the attention of the U.K. population.

The card works as a swipe card, and records the amount a customer spends on each transaction. A rebate of 1% of the total amount spent is offered to each customer.

The reaction from competitors

When market leader J. Sainsbury saw what Tesco had done, the scheme was immediately dismissed by the then chairman, David Sainsbury, as "electronic green shield stamps." He couldn't see that people would get excited about a meagre 1% rebate. But he missed the point on a number of fronts. Not only was 1% better than nothing, which was what Sainsbury's stores were giving, but it marked the beginning of a new era in grocery retailing—one where the store could once again build a knowledge of each individual customer and treat them differently. The card's introduction, coupled with the lack of foresight and of an adequate response by Sainsbury, allowed Tesco quickly to become the U.K.'s biggest supermarket group.

David Sainsbury eventually admitted that he was wrong in June 1996, when Sainsbury's launched its own card. But by then it was too late. The public just thought they were trying to copy Tesco. Sainsbury has being trying ever since to retake the initiative. Despite changes at Sainsbury at the chief executive level over the years, and a reworking of their Reward card program, Tesco has continued to be the market leader.

The mechanics of the Clubcard program

Let's have a detailed look at the workings of the Clubcard program itself.

Joining the Clubcard program

To participate in the scheme, a customer must "apply" for a Clubcard. This is a simple process where any person can pick up an application form in-store. The card is glued to the application form, so that there is no waiting time before it can be used. Customers are asked to write their name, address, and basic demographic details on the application form—just enough information for Tesco to be able to establish a basic customer record.

Data collection

The card has a magnetic stripe on its rear. Whenever a customer comes into the store and makes a purchase of £1 or more, the card is swiped at the point of sale and the points are registered against the customer's record. At the same time, the system is logging details of the specific purchases being made, down to individual stock-keeping units (SKU) data. This allows

Tesco to build a profile of how often an individual customer comes into a store, and which areas of the store they visit in the shop—for example, deli, fruit and vegetables, liquor. The swipe also records what they buy—if they buy beans, say, it records what brand they buy, what size can, how many cans, and so on.

This data is worth a fortune to Tesco for stock ordering and store planning purposes, not to mention the opportunities it provides to promote cross-selling and up-selling. In addition, the captured data is used to drive highly targeted marketing, such as invitations to events in local stores, and Tesco tries to send customers offers that are relevant in some way to them. The very best customers, the most profitable ones, receive invitations to events held at the store where the senior store personnel interact with them and develop personal relationships. We have heard that they are often invited to give feedback on new product lines and to share their ideas about store improvements.

The Clubcard scheme is used as a source of constant feedback by Tesco. It is truly a program based around dialogue with customers, and they seem to have got it right. According to David Perkins, Carlson Marketing Group's head of loyalty marketing, 83% of Tesco's Clubcard users think the frequency of contact is right and only 8% say they would like to hear from the store more often. This compares with only 67% of Sainsbury's Reward card users, with 18% wanting to hear from them more frequently.

Customer communications

Each Clubcard member receives a quarterly magazine. This is segmented into five variants: for students; for younger people without children; for shoppers with families; for older customers with children; and for pensioners. Along with the Clubcard magazine, members receive a statement showing their points balance.

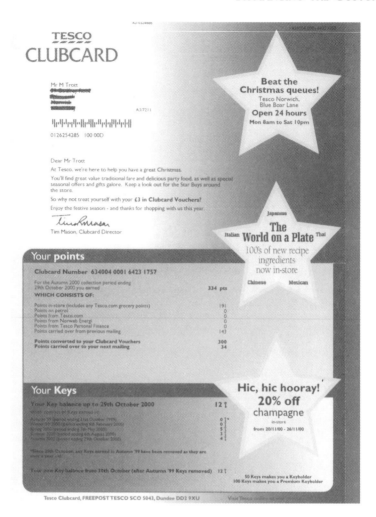

Customer reward

Customers also receive two sets of vouchers, which can only be used in conjunction with their Clubcard.

- The left-hand part of the voucher set consists of rebating points earned by the customer from the money they have already spent.

- The vouchers on the right-hand side are driven from the purchase data. Some offer discounts on products that Tesco

knows the customer regularly buys. Others try to tempt the customer to buy things from areas of the store that the data suggests the customer doesn't regularly go to. In this way, Tesco tries to grow its customers' shopping baskets.

Grant Harrison, the Clubcard coordinator, explains how they arrived at this format for the program. "From our point of view, Clubcard is an extension to customer service, and service is about the relationship with the customer. Clubcard gives us a chance to improve it. Direct mailing offers are very personal and give the customer the chance to think about them before going shopping. If the rewards were purely electronic, the customers would never have to tell you who they are. As it is, we get very direct communication."

Tesco decided on discounts, rather than other forms of reward, following feedback from market research. It was clear that customers wanted the flexibility to be able to choose something that would be of value to them. Tesco has a large range of products and is continually expanding the range of services it offers to customers, so there is always plenty to choose from.

The Clubcard program evolves—brand elasticity

Shortly after its initial launch, Tesco launched two card variants. One was aimed at students, offering a 2% rebate rather than the normal 1%. The other card, Clubcard Plus, represented Tesco's first foray into personal banking, allowing customers to deposit money into an account on which interest was paid. When in-store, customers merely present their Clubcard Plus card at the checkout and the money is deducted directly from their account.

In April 1996, Tesco linked Clubcard with the leading DIY retailer, B&Q. Whenever a Clubcard member bought goods in any of B&Q's 260 outlets, they also earned Clubcard points.

In 1997, Tesco introduced its Mother and Baby Club. The club offers mothers the chance to save up to £150 on a range of baby essentials and provides treats for the expectant mother. Mothers-to-be receive a sequence of eight magazines as they progress through the stages of their pregnancy. Tesco has also created special facilities at many of its stores for mothers with babies, including dedicated parking bays, changing and crèche facilities, and personal shoppers.

In the same year, Tesco expanded its range of financial services to include provision of mortgages, insurances, and a Tesco Visa card. In 1998, the deregulation of the U.K. utilities market saw electricity and telecoms being provided under the

Tesco brand. The company also has a partnership in place with GM Vauxhall to sell vehicles from Tesco's forecourts as soon as the regulators allow.

The company has negotiated deals with Eurostar, EuroDisney, Virgin Trains, KLM Royal Dutch Airlines, Aer Lingus, and many other companies to offer half-price airfares, train tickets, holidays, and theater and sporting tickets to Clubcard members. Through a partnership with British Telecom, Tesco has become an Internet ISP. This supports its move into Internet shopping, a move that has proved to be a roaring success. Contrast this with Tesco's sparring partner, Sainsbury's, which stopped its home-shopping trial outside of London's M25 ring road in mid-1999 after finding that too few shoppers wanted to use it.

Terry Leahy has said, "We will be the world's biggest online grocery retailer and we intend to become the U.K.'s No. 1 e-commerce business. We are now setting up warehouses that allow us to move into a massive range of books, CDs, and videos." He added that Tesco would "potentially" expand into electronic products. The drive into non-food-related items has had a very positive impact on the company's profits, Leahy said. "We wanted to push the business into retailing more than just food, for the obvious reason that higher consumer spending is on non-food, leisure, savings, and services."

The magnetic pull of the Tesco brand, activated and maintained through its CRM program, has been the main catalyst for brand stretch. The elasticity of the Tesco brand seems to be capable of infinite coverage, giving the company the opportunity and acceptance to go into whatever product categories and industries it wants.

In its latest evolution of Clubcard, Tesco is set to become the largest provider of leisure services in the U.K. Launched in August 1999, Tesco's Clubcard "keys" scheme means that every time a Clubcard holder spends £25 in the store, they are given a "key." Once a customer has earned 50 "keys," which means they will have spent £1,250 in-store, they become a

"Keyholder." As a Keyholder, the customer can take advantage of a range of half-price holidays, airfares, and cheap tickets to the theater and sporting events.

The discounts grow as the customer spends more with Tesco. Once the Keyholder has earned 100 keys (equivalent to £2,500 spent), they become a "Premium Keyholder" entitling them to a 75% discount on the services.

Tesco knows that more than 90% of their customers spend over £25 a week, so the scheme is open to the vast majority of its customers. In a really nice move, Tesco decided that all Clubcard holders over the age of 60, an estimated two million people, would automatically become Keyholders. All other existing Clubcard holders were given 25 keys each.

In its official press launch, a spokesman for Tesco said: "We have purchased over a million tickets for our customers. We now offer deals to EuroDisney and Haven holidays, and cheap tickets for all sorts of events. For example, customers will be able to go to France for a weekend in Monte Carlo, including hotel accommodation, for just £68. This really sets us apart from other schemes."

You can check out the enormous range of deals offered to Tesco customers by visiting www.tesco.com/clubcard/clubcardDeals.

Internal marketing

We have discussed the importance of internal marketing—that is, letting everyone who works within your organization know what your program is setting out to achieve, and how it will benefit customers and staff alike. When Clubcard was launched, Tesco gathered together all its store managers for a briefing by the main board. Tesco sees the involvement of all its 130,000 staff as critical to the success of Clubcard. Grant Harrison says, "Clubcard is part of Tesco now. A lot of effort has been put into communicating the scheme in ways relevant to them. It is a huge cascade."

In launching Clubcard Plus, Tesco achieved another first in its history, when every member of staff received a personal communication directly from the chairman. Installing a successful CRM program requires the commitment of the people at the top. This type of initiative typifies Tesco's refreshing thinking and absolute desire to ensure the success of Clubcard and enhance the brand image.

How Tesco uses Clubcard data

Recently, Sainsbury's appears to be taking a good hard look at its Reward card program, with a view to abandoning it on the basis of its running costs. Safeway, another of the U.K.'s grocery retailers, has already abandoned its ABC card for similar reasons. Why have these retailers questioned the cost of their programs, while Tesco would never consider such a move? We believe that the answer lies in the way Tesco turns the Clubcard data into immensely powerful knowledge that literally drives its business. Clubcard data is held centrally, but points information is held locally at the main stores used by a customer. This approach prevents Tesco becoming swamped by the sheer volume of data in the system.

Information is analyzed and fed back to the stores. "We are spending a lot of money on information, but we have to think a lot about what we want to do. We don't want information that's just nice to have; we want information that we'll act on."

Information is held at two levels: in a central management information system that all stores have access to; and in each store to support local marketing initiatives. For example, Tesco runs evenings at stores to which their most valued customers are invited. The evenings have specific themes, such as hair and cosmetics, or wine and cheese. Customers are selected for invitations from the Clubcard data based on their value to the store and declared areas of interest.

From the data it has, Tesco has worked out that at a typical store with 15,000 customers, the top 100 customers are worth more than the bottom 4,000. In revenue terms, a top-value customer will be worth £1,681 per year, a bottom customer £35. A mid-range customer might be worth £200. Given these values, would you agree that all customers are equal? No, and neither does Tesco, but it does believe that "every single customer is crucial."

Customers are categorized in a number of ways. One example is frequency of visits to the store. Labels such as "regular monthly" or "can't stay away" are used. This segmentation enables Tesco to compare the performance of one store with another with a similar customer frequency profile. It can also be used to understand the likely impact on a store's trading figures if a competitor began a price discount promotion. If a store had a large number of customers in the "can't stay away" category, then they would expect the impact to be lower than for a store with a weighting toward "infrequent" users.

Clubcard data is also used to drive store design. Data about which areas of the store customers visit is used to improve layout in order to encourage increased customer spending. It is no secret that retail store designers try to find layouts that maximize the likelihood of customers making impulse buys. Traditional thinking has been to place necessities at the point furthest away from the store entrance, so that customers have to make their way through the store to get what they need. Clubcard data enables the designers to analyze exactly which items are regularly purchased together, so increasing the precision of where they are distributed within the store. This has the dual effect of increasing the chances of customers making related impulse purchases, while also making the store easier for the customer to use.

There is no doubt in our minds that Tesco's Clubcard program data is the most fully utilized of any such program in the U.K., and probably in the world. Certainly, there is no other company in the U.K. retail market that has a better understanding of who its customers are and what they require from the organization.

Clubcard's contribution to the success of Tesco

In financial terms, the impact of Clubcard for Tesco has been substantial (see Table 6.1).

Table 6.1 Tesco results, 1994/95 to 1997/98

February 1994/95		February 1997/98
Market share 12%	⟶	15.6%
Sales £10.8 billion	⟶	£15.56 billion (44%)
Profit £578 million	⟶	£850 million (47%)
Like-for-like sales 1998/99 up 5% against industry average 1.5%		

The launch of Clubcard helped Tesco, within three years of launch, to increase its market share by 3.6%, its sales by 44%, and its profits by 47%. These are substantial numbers, achieved in a fully matured market. Most of the increase in market share was taken away from Sainsbury's.

But Tesco's success hasn't stopped there. It has gone from strength to strength. In December 1999, it was named as Britain's most admired company for a record third time, and for the second consecutive year by *Management Today*. Year 2000 saw a price war among the leading supermarkets in the U.K., but even against this backdrop, analysts expect Tesco's profit to rise to £1.065 billion pre-tax for the year ending February 2001. David McCarthy, a food retailing analyst with investment bank Schroder Salamon Smith Barney, commenting on Tesco's sales performance, says: "Tesco is outgrowing Sainsbury's by over £1 billion p.a." Tesco announced that sales at its U.K. stores rose by 8.9%.

Increasing focus on non-food products is no doubt contributing to this continued sales growth, but it does seem that Tesco is unstoppable. Even the takeover of Asda stores by America's Wal-Mart has had little impact on the undisputed king of U.K. retailing. Tesco is now aggressively expanding in Asia and looks destined to become a global brand.

Case Study 12
BOOTS THE CHEMIST
World-class CRM in action

Boots The Chemist is U.K.'s leading health and beauty retailer. Ninety percent of the U.K.'s 60 million population visits a Boots store at least once a year. The company has an annual turnover of around £3 billion from a network of some 1,300 stores.

In the early 1990s, when the retailing sector jumped on to the bandwagon of loyalty cards, Boots initially kept a watching brief. Boots' reasoning was, "We took time developing our scheme to make sure it was different to other schemes, but more importantly, so that it fitted in with our brand image and it was right for the company, our customers, and shareholders." Many retailers, seeing the emergence of Tesco's highly successful Clubcard program, felt that they had no choice but to take the plunge.

Boots first began planning a loyalty card in November 1993, but what they built is much more than a loyalty card; it is a very full CRM program. From humble beginnings, and with an investment in excess of £30 million, the Boots Advantage Card is the largest smart card retail loyalty card scheme in the world. It is also the third-largest retail loyalty scheme in the U.K. in terms of cards issued. The Advantage scheme currently has 12.3 million cardholders, and more than 40% of transactions in-store are now linked to the card.

Prior to the national launch, Boots ran two trials in two cities. The trials provided Boots with invaluable information and allowed them to fine-tune the program to maximize its financial contribution to the business before the decision was made to roll it out nationally.

By analyzing the information provided through the Advantage Card, Boots gained meaningful insights into its customers' shopping behavior. It found that Advantage cardholders shop more frequently than non-cardholders, and on average spend 50% more than non-cardholders.

The target market for the Advantage Card is females (83% of Boots' customers are female) aged 20–45. Research led Boots to create a positioning for the program of "Pure Indulgence." The personalized card enables customers to treat themselves to something special, instead of reducing the cost of their normal shopping. The basic reward rate for the Advantage Card is 4% (four points for every £1 spent). This is a very generous rate of reward compared to the other retail sectors. The major supermarket discount cards reward only 1%, and the high street stationery retailer W.H. Smith rewards 2%. There is no minimum spend, so a spend of 24p will still earn one point. Cardholders get to treat themselves from a selection of over 10,000 different items and services as rewards, including a range of health and beauty treatments. Redemption can be made at the checkout in any Boots store, as opposed to some schemes that require redemption at the local store only.

The program is supported by regular mailings, offers, and double-points promotions, which have helped to push membership to its current level.

The Advantage Card now represents one of the largest loyalty schemes in Europe. It continues to be an integral part of the Boots marketing effort, with Boots' own-brand opticians stores being added to the scheme. Two million cardholders now receive a quarterly *Health and Beauty* magazine, making it the largest-circulation female interest magazine. This has created a medium for Boots to demonstrate its expertise in the health and beauty market.

In September 1999, Boots launched "The Advantage Point" in stores. These are interactive kiosks that enable cardholders to view personally tailored offers and incentives by inserting their Advantage Card into the terminal. This creates a real feeling of interacting with the program, as well as another reason to visit the store.

The Advantage Point is taking this type of program to another level. Instead of Boots deciding which vouchers to send to the cardholder, it is left to the customer to decide which ones are relevant at the time they are in-store.

Also in September 1999, Boots announced the launch of its Advantage credit card, in conjunction with Egg, the online financial services company. The card is the first of its kind in Europe, using smart chip technology such that a single card can manage the Advantage Card loyalty scheme, Europay, MasterCard, and Visa (EMV) payment simultaneously.

"The launch of the card extends the Advantage Card proposition beyond Boots stores," comments Steve Murphy, head of Advantage credit card at Boots. Richard Duvall, chief marketing officer at Egg, comments: "The card offers consumers great interest rates and special deals on balance transfers, combined with the benefits of a proven loyalty scheme from one of the U.K.'s leading retailers. This is the first initiative of its kind in Europe and we anticipate that it will be a great success."

In a few short years, there is no doubt that Boots has built one of the most successful CRM programs we have seen. It waited, sensibly, to see what the high street competition did. It then researched the program with its customers, and ran a trial to fine-tune as necessary before the final massively successful roll-out. You can see the product yourself at www.boots.co.uk.

7

Making Your Brand More Customer-focused

In this chapter, we will first take you through the financial aspects of CRM program planning, so that you will be able to forecast and monitor the impact of the program on company profitability. Having discussed this area, we will then present a case study that shows how we helped implement a complete CRM program using the methodology we have advocated in the book so far. At the end of the chapter, we hope you will have a good understanding of how CRM can benefit your company by making it more customer-focused, and by acting as a catalyst to your brand-building or brand repositioning efforts.

WORKING OUT THE FINANCIAL CASE FOR THE PROJECT

We could easily devote an entire chapter to the financial justification for your CRM project, but all we really want to do is give you a feel for the type of model we would expect you to create to justify your project in financial terms. Bearing this in mind, we will walk you through some of the costs you need to cover, and how you can illustrate the positive impact on the business, but you will no doubt work with your financial division to build this. They may well want to go into a lot more depth than this for their own purposes, but a simplistic model will be sufficient for your own purposes in planning and building your CRM program.

A worked illustration

Let's imagine we are a retail company wanting to embark on a CRM program. We have undertaken our audit and found that we have details of around 50,000 customers in various systems, and we want to use this as the starting point for our program. Our ambition is to create a reward and recognition CRM program. We will create an application form and take the opportunity to ask for a few pieces of lifestyle data we need for later marketing activity. As a carrot, we will offer customers who join the program a refund of 1% of everything they spend in the store in the form of store vouchers.

Each quarter we will send customers a brief newsletter, telling them about new products and services at our store, and enclosing their vouchers for what they have spent. We will give customers a card to present to earn and redeem the points, and they will be able to enrol on the spot in-store. The existing 50,000 customers will automatically be enrolled, and will be sent a card and questionnaire to complete so that we can update the data we hold about them.

What might the project cost justification look like for this scenario? Have a look at the spreadsheet below.

Sheet 1: Program Overview

Financial Analysis of Sample CRM Program

Sales projections	Year 1 $000	Year 2 $000	Year 3 $000
Sales projected without CRM program	100,000	110,000	120,000
Average gross profit margin	20%	20%	20%
Profit	20,000	22,000	24,000
Profit contribution of CRM program			
Assumed impact of CRM program	5%	5%	5%
Revised sales projection with CRM installed	105,000	115,500	126,000
Revised profit projection	21,000	23,100	25,200

	Year 1 '000	Year 2 '000	Year 3 '000
Projected increase in gross profit	1,000	1,100	1,200
Costs of CRM program			
Ongoing costs (see Sheet 2 for details)			
Documentation	249	249	249
Despatch/mailing	100	100	100
Award points	105	105	105
One-off costs (see Sheet 3 for details)			
Advertising	38		
Creative work	5		
Launch PR	4		
Mailing to existing customer database	5		
Consultancy costs	50		
Total CRM program costs	556	414	414
Projected increase in gross profit	1,000	1,100	1,200
Net gain through CRM installation	**444**	**686**	**786**

For this purpose, we have taken a three-year view, which is sufficient for most companies; however, if you are used to working with a five-year view, just extend the model.

The impact on sales and profits:
- Start by looking at projected sales for the next three years—this is the current projection ignoring the impact of your CRM efforts.
- Next, find out what the average gross profit margin is for those divisions, areas, or products encompassed by your program. Here we have used a figure of 20%. If there are wild variances in the profit margins by division or product, work out the individual figures and total them. Work out your projected profit in dollar value.
- Now you need to make an estimate of the impact your CRM program will have on your business. How much do you think you can grow the

turnover of the business by getting closer to the customer, growing the customer's loyalty to your brand, actively marketing to them things that you know they need, cross-selling goods and services you know they need, and offering them options to trade up to better products? Think not only of the extra goods and services you are likely to sell, but also about what the financial impact would be if you reduced the rate at which customers defected from you by a few percentage points.

For this illustration, we have suggested an improvement on turnover of 5%. You may feel that this is low, and it might well be, but it is best not to start out by making outlandish claims that take away from the plan. Accountants take a lot of convincing sometimes, especially when it comes to claims of extra sales by the marketing division! Make reasonable statements and support them with workings wherever you can get the numbers.

- Returning to the numbers, an increase on projected profits in year 1 would see this company increase its projected sales from $100 million to $105 million, and its projected profits from $20 million to $21 million—an increase of $1 million profit directly attributable to the CRM activity.

The impact on costs:
- Next, we need to look at what it will cost to earn that $1 million extra profit.
- There are two sets of potential costs—those that are incurred on an ongoing basis, and those that are specific to the program launch and are therefore a one-off cost.
- Looking at the ongoing costs first, consider:
  - **Documentation**: Work out what documents you are going to need to run the program. We have allowed for an application form, questionnaires, membership cards, letterheads and envelopes, and a reply envelope for the return of the questionnaires.
  - **Fulfillment costs**: These are the costs of actually sending out your documents. If you use external resources, there is a charge per piece handled to pull together the letter and card and put them into an envelope. You also need to allow for the relevant postage costs.

- ○ **Quarterly letter**: You will also need to allow for your quarterly letter. For instance, if you have 100,000 customers in your program, that will be 400,000 mailings per year.
- ○ **Award points**: Finally, you must account for your award points, and we offer a word of advice here. Make sure that you put a finite life on your award points—in other words, give the customer a date by which they must use them. There are two reasons for this, the first of which is financial. A finite life means your accountants won't have the problem of having to carry forward thousands of unclaimed points each year. Second, from a marketing point of view, it ensures that people are motivated to come back to the store to use the vouchers, which will inevitably mean they have to buy more goods. In our example, we have taken a value of one award point for every $10 spent. It is important not to forget that, like all vouchers, only a percentage of them will be redeemed, as some people won't bother to do this. However, hopefully a high percentage will be redeemed, as that means your CRM program is successful but that there will also be some "savings" against your plan from unused vouchers.

- Now consider the one-off costs. In this area, you want to list any costs that are specific to the launch that aren't going to be incurred year on year. In this example, we have included items for advertising, the design work for the membership card and stationery, some public relations activity, the mail-out to the existing 50,000 customers, and some external consultancy (which could include the research costs). Adding all these costs together in our model for year 1 gives a total of $556,000.

The impact on the bottom line:
- Subtract the $556,000 costs from your projected gain in profit of $1 million to get a net positive impact on the bottom line of $444,000.
- For years 2 and 3, go through a similar process, but obviously exclude the one-off costs.

To understand the detail of how we worked out our costs, look at the following spreadsheets.

Sheet 2: Detailed Breakdown of Ongoing Costs

Ongoing costs	Quantity	Cost/unit	Total cost $
1. Documentation			
Application form	200,000	0.13	26,000
Questionnaires	100,000	0.15	15,000
Membership card	150,000	0.98	147,000
Envelopes	100,000	0.23	23,000
Letterhead	100,000	0.2	20,000
Reply envelope	100,000	0.18	18,000
		Total	**249,000**
2. Despatch/mailing			
Letter/points statement	400,000	0.1	40,000
Questionnaires	100,000	0.1	10,000
Postage	500,000	0.1	50,000
		Total	**100,000**
3. Award points			
	Contribution	Rate	Cost $
Award points	105,000,000	1%	**105,000**
(Assume 1 point for			
every $10 spent)			

Sheet 3: Detailed Breakdown of One-off Costs

One-off costs	
Service	Cost $
1. Advertising	
Ad production	7,500
Press advertisements	30,000
2. Creative work	
Cards & print material	5,000
3. Launch public relations activity	4,000
4. Mailing to existing customer database	5,000
(50,000 × 0.1)	
5. Consultancy costs	50,000
Total	**101,500**

We hope that the above explanatory example gives you a reasonable feel for how to approach your own costing exercise. There is no right and wrong way; it is merely a question of putting together something that both you and your financial team feel comfortable with, and against which you can track your actual outcome to see how well you did.

Understanding and owning your own model is important. Owning the numbers means that you will keep focused on the costs and not get carried away spending on things that may be "nice to have." And showing good progress against the plan early on will ensure that you receive all the support and resources you need to fully implement your CRM initiative.

INSTALLING A CRM PROGRAM TO REPOSITION YOUR BRAND

We have explained the basic process of developing your customer relationship blueprint, but what you really need to know is: What does it all mean in practice? How do you take the knowledge you have gained and apply it to your company? In Case Study 13, we have taken a company that had certain business and brand image concerns which needed to be addressed. Repositioning a brand is no easy task, especially when consumer perceptions are deeply entrenched, but a well thought-through CRM program can be a real catalyst to success in such circumstances.

Case Study 13

EON MALAYSIA
Brand repositioning in the motor industry

This example relates to the motor industry, where we worked for a year alongside EON, the national car distributor for Proton cars in Malaysia.

Introduction

Before the financial crisis of 1997, the tiger economies of Asia were showing significant year-on-year growth—8% being a fairly typical figure. Asia also, as we all now know, was living off an increasing credit line, which for the car industry meant an endless stream of customers regularly renewing their cars and adding a second or even third car. This apparent luxury had been going on for years, to the extent that there were waiting lists for cars to be supplied from the manufacturer—six months for a typical mainstream model, and even longer for specific color or trim options.

What this meant was that salespeople had ceased to be salespeople. They didn't have to put any real effort into the sales process, as customers were queuing up to buy cars. All the salespeople had to do was fill in the order form and tell the customer how long they could expect to wait.

For anyone in Asia in 1996 intending to buy a first car, the brand experience at the motorcar sales offices was hard to believe. Salespeople weren't the least bit interested in whether they sold a car or not, and demonstration cars weren't available. (No test drive before you buy!) There was no choice of color, and the most common response was: "We may have a car for you in about three months." For people who were new arrivals from developed countries, this was similar to landing on an alien planet. In the U.K. at that time, for example, if you walked into a showroom with cash in your hand, salespeople would be dropping at your feet, but this wasn't the case in Asia.

Having bought a car, when it came time for the first service, the service centers were an inconvenient distance away, and trying to get a taxi to go there was nigh on impossible. Not only that, but typically a company would want the car for a whole day to undertake a service, whereas a standard service, according to the manual, was at most one hour of work. Customers had to get to a service center early in the morning to stand any chance of their car being looked at that day, find their own way to work, and then find their own way back in the evening in the hope the job had been finished!

One of the larger car distributors wanted to improve the brand experience, and we were lucky enough to be appointed by Edaran Otomobil Nasional Berhad (EON), the distributor of Malaysia's national car, the Proton. The brief we had was to focus on one particular model—the top-of-the-range 2,000cc model called the Perdana—which was proving difficult to sell. Our challenge was to add some value to ownership of the car to help justify the additional cost of ownership of that model. In Malaysia at that time, once the engine size exceeded 1,800cc, there were sizable additional taxes to pay over and above the extra cost of servicing the car, and a 50% premium on the purchase price over the next model down the line.

We bought one of these cars to try it for ourselves and to get into the mindset of a typical owner. It was a very good car, great value for money against the competition, and it was being aimed at the up-and-coming business person and families who needed a slightly larger car.

Once we began interacting with the company as an owner, we were convinced that there were a number of initiatives which could be undertaken that would give some really quick wins, as well as some long-term initiatives. From talking to staff, we were soon aware that there was no ongoing relationship with customers. They came to buy a car and then went away, until they came back to buy another car. The general feeling was that many people had their cars serviced at non-franchised workshops to save money, and we investigated this later.

While our brief was to focus on the Perdana, we felt that the ideas we had would inevitably have positive impacts on the company as a whole, and therefore would benefit pretty much each and every customer. But we had to keep some exclusivity for owners of the top-of-the-line model. We were fortunate in that EON was part of a much larger conglomerate called DRB Hicom, which also owned an airline, a bank, an insurance company, and many other subsidiaries. This gave us a great backdrop to plan a CRM program that not only addressed the key issues for EON, but also began to cross-sell within the parent group.

This is an area we will talk about more in the next chapter. Partnership marketing, or the formation of alliances with other non-competitive organizations for marketing purposes, enables you to extend the brand range of products or services offered to your customers without growing your core business. It enables you to create more reasons for your customer to stay loyal to your brand, while enabling you to earn more from your customer base.

Shortly after we began work, Asia was thrown into economic turmoil. Overnight, there was virtually no finance available, and car sales dropped steeply. Consequently, and very suddenly, the idea of being able to make money from existing customers became of acute interest to our client and other companies, and we were now under pressure to deliver!

The process

Here is a detailed description of the process we went through.

Step 1: Auditing the systems

We were invited into the IT department and met with the IT director with whom we talked at a high level about the sorts of things we were likely to need to do. We obtained an overview of the various systems within the company, what their functions were, which platforms they ran on, and how the systems talked to each other. We also asked for an initial identification of which systems were likely to be holding customer data.

For our needs, there were two key systems as far as we could tell: sales and after-sales. The sales system had records of orders placed by customers, and details of the vehicles delivered. We could obtain customer names, addresses, and possibly telephone numbers. It also held the vehicle registration number for the delivered vehicles. The after-sales system held information relevant to the servicing of the vehicles, including name and address, registration number, and a few details about the car, such as mileage at the last service and when the next service was due.

The two systems sat on different platforms, and data was only passed from one to another if the after-sales system requested details of a particular vehicle. In other words, you could buy a car today and the after-sales department wouldn't know you existed until you went into the workshop for your first service. Then, when your vehicle details were keyed into the after-sales system, if it couldn't find your details it would retrieve them from the sales system.

Here was our first major opportunity for the company. If the after-sales team could be aware of cars going out of the showroom, and proactively contact customers to ensure they came back to the company for the first service (and subsequent services) instead of going to other independent service centers, it would be the first chance to maintain the relationship with the customer. However, it was also about to become our first major project issue. We were told that there were few resources available in the IT shop, because of work needing to be done to deal with potential Y2K bug fallout (remember that?) and they were taking the opportunity to install an entirely new set of systems. This meant that we were pretty much on our own to provide systems support.

Having been made aware of the new systems initiative, we asked to see the marketing specifications for the new system. You probably won't be surprised to hear that as the IT department was specifying the new system and there was no dialogue under way with the marketing division, there was pretty much nothing in the new system to help marketing move forward in any way. By the time we arrived, it was too late to do anything about this situation and the required marketing functionality was committed to "Phase 2." "Phase 2" in IT lexicon tends to mean "something we'll get away with not doing unless we're really made to." If you are in a similar situation and have to concede your function to a Phase 2, make sure that it is a planned Phase 2, with a budget and resources available to make it a reality, and don't sign off on Phase 1 without that commitment.

Step 2: Auditing the data

The IT team gave us access to the list of data items available. There were plenty of items, but, unfortunately, too many of them weren't compulsory inputs, so we had a lot of holes in the data. In addition, much of the sales data was as much as three years old, and we had no way of knowing if it was still correct. For example, did the person who bought the car still own it? We would have to address these issues.

There was a healthy degree of overlap between the data on the sales system and the after-sales system, which gave us some heart. By running the two files against each other, we thought we might be able to fill in some gaps and validate some of the vehicle ownership details. For instance, if a customer had brought in the vehicle recently for a service, we could validate the owner's name against the sales database, joining the two databases on registration number.

Because of the resource limits within the IT department, we built a small database using Microsoft Access to undertake the merging and analysis work. The IT department merely needed to give us a dump of the data from the two systems. Not only did this speed things up, but it enabled us to run a number of queries on the data, which we will comment on when we talk about the financial case. It also gave us the beginnings of our marketing database, which is the heart of any CRM initiative.

Step 3: Auditing existing customer relationships

Malaysia is a country with massive national pride. Loyalty to the national car project was, and is, incredibly strong, and EON as the distributor were benefiting significantly from this. Depending on the model they wanted to buy, customers really had no choice but to deal with EON as distributor, but EON knew that it couldn't rely on this always being the case and was keen to try and develop a stronger relationship with its customers. The company already ran a small customer hotline within the marketing division, which took details of problems and complaints, all of which were responded to and logged, and this gave us a good feel for some of the concerns being expressed by customers. But we wanted to learn more.

We undertook some basic research with customers by mailing out a questionnaire to all the Perdana model owners. As we were mailing to existing customers, we pre-filled the questionnaire with the data we already held, and merely asked customers to correct anything that was wrong and fill in any blanks. As we have pointed out previously, questionnaires don't have to be bland black-and-white rows of tick-boxes. Taking a little more time over your questionnaire sends a signal that you are serious about what you are doing and that you intend to make good use of the information the customer provides. The style of the questionnaire we used is shown on the next page:

We installed a questionnaire "helpline" in our offices that customers could call if they needed any guidance. We answered it as EON, so as far as the customers were concerned, we *were* EON.

Pre-filling the questionnaire, thinking carefully about its design, and providing an incentive for its return rewarded us with a response rate of 28%. Customers had gone to a lot of trouble to fully complete the questionnaire, and many had sent in supplementary pages to give feedback on areas where they would like to see improvements made. Here are some of the key findings:

- The remote location of the servicing center was an issue. The company already had a minibus to ferry people to designated drop-off points, but this wasn't really seen as a suitable solution.

- There was also too much waiting around at the center. The service reception used a "Q-matic" system, where customers took a number and waited to be attended to. But customers couldn't understand why it wasn't possible to book the car in for a service at a specific time. After all, these same people were used to having an appointment at their doctor or dentist. Why wasn't it possible to designate a time for the car to be serviced? Why did the service center need the car for so long? A typical service takes 60–90 minutes, but the car had to be there all day. These were all reasonable questions from clearly frustrated customers.

- Customers didn't like the impersonal service. They complained that they "never saw the same person twice" when they came to the main distributor, and so preferred to take their vehicles to small workshops where they always saw the same mechanic, who knew the car and understood

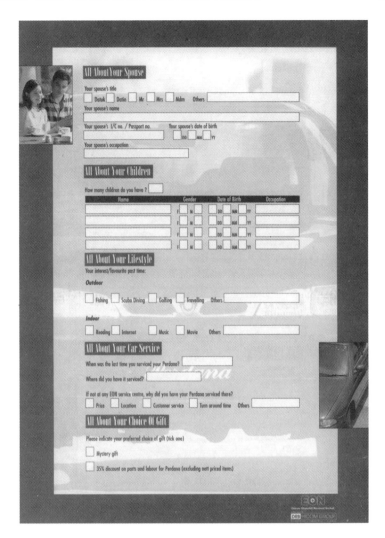

its history. This meant they didn't have to explain everything over and over.

- There were concerns about the quality of the workmanship. Customers had the impression of the car mechanics being "young kids," and of course everyone wanted to think that their car was worked on by an experienced mechanic.

- We were able to identify that there were problems ringing into the company. The main switchboard was strictly 9 to 5. After that time, it was unlikely that the calls would be answered, and it was also hard to get a phone answered on a Saturday morning. Our questionnaire helpline started to become a general helpline once customers knew it was answered immediately. Customers always find the path of least resistance! This was actually very helpful, and we were able to ring into the relevant contacts in the group and help to get matters resolved.

- One of the biggest things we learned was that customers didn't feel that their problems were being owned by anyone in EON. What they wanted was an individual to take ownership and manage them through their difficulties to a conclusion.

- We were also able to identify a number of problems with the product itself. There were recurring stories of air-conditioning failures, gearbox noise, and problems with the CD player/radio. This was all fed back to EON and on to the manufacturer, Proton. Some of these were known problems and were already being addressed for the revised model, but it was useful feedback, and customers appreciated the fact that they were being listened to.

- Through raising questions about the component failures on the product, we also learned that the majority of the components of these cars were covered by a five-year warranty—this was powerful marketing information. Most owners didn't appreciate this, and once the 12-month stage warranty they thought they had had expired, they were going off to non-franchise workshops.

Step 4: Auditing the financials

Having loaded the data on to our database, and merged the sales and after-sales data, we began to analyze what it was telling us. The data suggested that only one in six vehicles that left the showroom were currently coming back to the workshop for a service. Less than 5% were coming in for services to the manufacturer's correct schedule. This meant that there was significant business for the workshop to go for.

On average, cars were coming in for servicing every six months or so, but in the Malaysian tropical climate, the manufacturers recommended that the service interval should be three months. We also noticed a marked extension of the servicing intervals as soon as the economy started to slow, which was impacting on revenues.

Therefore we had a significant block of revenue to go for, as five out of every six cars could potentially be attracted back to EON for servicing, and those customers who were already coming back could be persuaded to visit more regularly.

Having established what the average cost of servicing was, and an average profit margin, we were able quickly to calculate the extra revenue potential set against the cost of the project. The numbers worked out well, the project was approved, and we got under way.

Step 5: Creating a CRM strategy

One of the things that intrigues us about the motor industry, and this is probably true anywhere in the world, is that the after-sales division always seems to be the "Cinderella" of the company. The sales team appears to get all the glamor and the perks, while the after-sales team is left to deal with pretty much all the problems and complaints. And yet, typically a person only buys a new car every three years or so, but they have it serviced at least every six months, so when you look at which team is the more important in terms of being able to maintain and build the customer relationship, the way that most dealerships work it is the after-sales division that should get more rewards and recognition! This can be true in other sectors too, from mortgages to mobile phones.

Financially, too, we all know how important sales of parts are in determining profits to manufacturers and dealerships. It was certainly true within EON that the after-sales division felt under-appreciated. We wanted to propagate a culture of "Service is the greatest sales tool we have." We wanted everyone working within the company to see that by dedicating themselves to serving the customer, they could increase sales, profits, and brand image.

Above all, we wanted EON's customers and prospective customers to see a company who understood what people needed and actually responded to those needs. EON needed to be seen as the company that understood their customers better than the cars they were driving. They wanted to become a company that people *wanted to* do business with, not just *had to*. This was the key brand repositioning issue that needed to be addressed.

Building the blueprint. We had built a profile of the typical Perdana owner, who turned out to be a 30 to 45-year-old businessman, married with children, who was fairly dependent on a car to be able to run his business and to whom time was money. The "Perdana Person" was on the way to becoming successful in life, and bought a Perdana to demonstrate their achievement and success. They were looking for an outward demonstration of their career or business achievement.

From all the findings we had to hand, we then built up our blueprint, as shown in Figure 7.1.

Step 6: Creating tactical CRM programs

We found that Perdana owners were interested in being rewarded, but they were more interested in receiving benefits and privileges that would make them feel special and save them time.

The Premier Lounge. We mentioned earlier about reusing initiatives wherever possible. EON had already started to look at ways to enhance the Perdana ownership experience, and was in the process of launching a "Premier Lounge" for Perdana owners. This was a separate lounge attached to the service center, which looked more like a first class lounge at an airport. It was lavishly furnished, with soft sofas and a TV, and a fresh coffee maker, so that customers and their families could relax while they waited for their car to be worked on.

Customers liked the facility, but when we sat and talked with a few of them while they waited, it was clear that a comfortable wait was no substitute for getting the car serviced quickly so that they could get back to work, or wherever else they wanted to go.

We picked up on the "Premier" title of the lounge, and developed it into a discrete service level all the way through the company. Customers who already owned or had bought a Perdana model in the past automatically became Perdana "Premier" cardholders.

The Premier Card. The card was the face of a CRM strategy that we developed for EON which rewarded customers for the money they were currently spending, while trying to encourage them to spend more, particularly at the service center. But more importantly, it gave Premier customers access to a range of unique services, designed to remove the hassle

Figure 7.1: The EON CRM blueprint

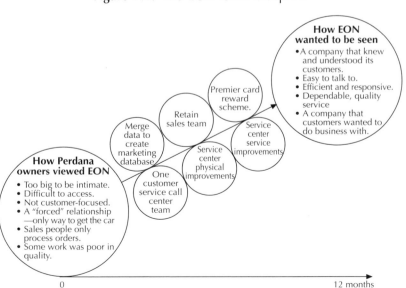

How EON wanted to be seen
- A company that knew and understood its customers.
- Easy to talk to.
- Efficient and responsive.
- Dependable, quality service
- A company that customers wanted to do business with.

Premier card reward scheme.

Retain sales team

Service center service improvements

Merge data to create marketing database

Service center physical improvements

How Perdana owners viewed EON
- Too big to be intimate.
- Difficult to access.
- Not customer-focused.
- A "forced" relationship —only way to get the car
- Sales people only process orders.
- Some work was poor in quality.

One customer service call center team

0   12 months

from dealing with the service center and to speed up the process, which meant that having their car serviced created as little disruption as possible to their normal daily lives. This was seen as important, as it was a major deterrent factor to using the EON service center.

The privileges. The privileges we worked alongside EON to install were as follows:

- The "Premier Lounge" service was extended to any member of a family owning a Perdana. Even if you were having a different model serviced, because you had a Perdana in the family, you were entitled to use the lounge. This created a family privilege, and a compelling reason to keep a Perdana in the family!

- A new role of service consultant was created. These were senior mechanics who were made EON's single point of contact for the customer at the service center. The service consultant was responsible for checking the car in and out, and performing a quality check on the mechanic's work before releasing it to the customer. We introduced a system to proactively contact the customer and book their car in for a service when their particular service consultant was on shift, to maintain the continuity.

   This initiative addressed a number of the key customer concerns. First, the lack of intimacy when dealing with a large workshop was avoided by having customers meet the same service consultant each time, and this brought the entire workshop down to a single individual with whom a bond could be built. Second, it meant that the customer no longer had to give the car's life story to a different mechanic each time. Third, because the service consultant was taking ownership of the work on the vehicle and performing a quality check, concerns about the perceived inexperience of the mechanics went away.

From the information provided by customers via the questionnaires, we identified a number of new CRM initiatives and problem areas that needed addressing.

- We had to address the issue of the remote location of the EON service center. An initiative was launched to look at the viability of running a pick-up and delivery service, as we had established that several of the smaller workshops provided this type of facility. EON felt that this was likely to be too labor-intensive. It would be investigated, but we needed a quick win.

  We then thought about the possibility of providing a loan car to the customer while their car was being serviced. We talked to the marketing team about sponsoring a small fleet of cars to be offered to customers on a "first come, first served" basis. We had a number of thoughts in mind in heading down this path:

  o For the marketing team, it was a chance to put an existing Perdana owner into the very latest model and give them a teasing taste of a better model. In the circles these customers were moving in, being seen to have the latest and the best was socially important, and our feeling was that this might drive a few trade-up sales. Details of who had taken the loan car could be passed through to sales for a follow-up sales contact.

  o We knew the service center was installing a service booking system and wanted to encourage usage of the new facility. The more people who used the facility, the easier it was going to be to plan shift sizes in the workshop, with corresponding savings in manpower costs. By giving priority access to the loan cars to customers who pre-booked, we were able to encourage use of the facility.

- We worked alongside the EON team to install a number of new "high-speed" service lanes. These were special service bays equipped to allow a mechanic to undertake a routine service, lube change, plugs, and so on, within 30 minutes. We promoted this service by mail-shot directly to the customers, to show that EON was able to turn cars around quickly. Using this facility, it was quite possible for customers to book a service, come in, sit down in the lounge and enjoy a cup of coffee and a newspaper, by which time their car would be ready for collection.

- A new customer service call center team was put together. These people were picked from each of the divisions of the company, to ensure they could answer any question a customer might raise. They became the first point of contact for customers, removing the function from the corporate switchboard and the service center reception. As well as fielding inbound calls, the team also had a number of outbound calls to make:

  o Proactive calls to customers as their car fell due for its next service—to book the car into the service center at a convenient time for the customer.

  o Post-service courtesy calls—was everything OK with the car? Was the service completed to the customer's satisfaction?

  o Calls to the customer once their car's service was complete and the car was ready for collection.

- We also wanted to create a sense of teamwork between sales and after-sales. We detected a sense of "us and them," which wasn't healthy for the brand–customer relationship. To do this, we introduced the notion of "customer handover" by the salesperson to the after-sales team. When a customer came to collect their new car, the salesperson would take the customer through to meet the after-sales team, tour the workshops, and introduce them to the people who would be looking after them "from now on."

  We say "from now on," because there was one issue that needed to be tackled. This was the fact that salespeople had, up until now, tended to wash their hands of any problems the customer had with the car once it had left the forecourt. If something went wrong with the car, as can happen even with the best pre-delivery checks, customers were being directed to the after-sales division. This was destroying two relationships. From the customer's point of view, it came across as "you only want to look after me until you've got my money," and the after-sales team were getting tired of having to deal with upset customers who really ought to be being placated by the person they had built a relationship with—the salesperson. This issue was resolved by an agreement that salespeople should own any problem that arose with the vehicle within the first month, after which time the after-sales team would take responsibility.

- We analyzed the data within the after-sales system and identified vehicles for the sales team which had reached a certain mileage, or where the customer was likely to be coming toward the end of their financing arrangement. This was seen to be a good time to talk to the customer about renewing their car.

- We worked with the EON human resources team to run training workshops to refresh the sales teams in topics from prospecting for customers, to building long-term relationships with customers, and useful techniques to help close sales.

- EON also began to run "family fun weekends" at their head office to encourage customers to bring their families to look at various displays of cars and accessories, enjoy some refreshments, and tour the workshops and facilities—all of which served not only to attract customers to EON, but also to show them as a warm and accessible company.

CONCLUSION

By analyzing this particular case study, we hope that it has helped you to see the way to turn theory into practice. Hopefully, by now, you will have come up with ideas about what you might do within your own company to make a difference for your customers. You will have seen that CRM should be intuitive. The best yardstick against which to judge any customer service delivery is merely this: if you were in your customer's shoes, what would *you* want to happen, and what could you reasonably expect?

We recall seeing a *Harvard Business Review* video case study on MBNA, the affinity credit card issuer. One part of the case study stuck in our minds. At the head office of MBNA, sewn into every carpet, above every doorway, in each and every place a member of staff would sit or walk, was this simple maxim: "Think of yourself as a customer."

This maxim encapsulates the ideal mindset for anyone in customer service or marketing. If you understand what the customer would expect from you in any given situation, and find ways of delivering it, you won't go wrong. Approach your CRM from this viewpoint and you cannot fail to improve the overall performance of your organization. By focusing on your customer, sales will increase, your brand will become stronger, and your corporate image will improve tremendously.

8

Final Steps and Touches

In this chapter, we will discuss the final touches you can put to your CRM program, and how you should make sure that your brand value is increasing. In particular, we would like to mention the ways in which you can really add value to your brand by linking up with other companies in CRM partnership arrangements. We will also touch on how important it is to track the fortunes of your brand and your CRM program.

ADDING VALUE THROUGH CRM PARTNERSHIP ARRANGEMENTS

Over the last five years or so, formation of marketing partnerships has become big business. Existing agencies have seen the earning potential and many new agencies have emerged, dedicating themselves to the role. Partnership marketing can be seen as a corollary of CRM. It has emerged from the realization that a company's customer database is an asset to be mined, and there is good money to be earned by selling more goods and services to existing customers.

Partnership marketing is the bringing together of two or more companies for the purpose of marketing goods or services to create competitive advantage and generate incremental revenues for all involved. There are two approaches a company can take to achieve this: it can extend its core business to include other goods and services (which means pushing up costs); or it can form partnerships with other non-competing companies (which means less cost and more revenue).

171

LEVERAGING BRAND TRUST AND PRODUCT AWARENESS

We talked in Chapter 6 about the concept of brand elasticity—that is, understanding what additional products your current brand positioning would allow you to sell. Importantly, what will your customers give you permission to sell to them? Perhaps the most important factor in the ability of any company to extend its brand is trust. The compelling truth is that *people trust brands, and great brands are built on trust*. Without consumer trust, your brand will go nowhere.

Creating a high degree of trust in your brand and organization is key to securing the loyalty of your customers over the long term. Companies that manage to attain high levels of trust can successfully extend their brands into other areas. Some well-known brands that have taken this route include:

- British Airways (financial services);
- Tesco (financial services, utility services, Internet ISP);
- Virgin (cola, mobile phones, financial services, trains, cosmetics, airlines, and many more);
- Boots (financial services); and
- Sony (consumer electronics, entertainment).

It is happy customers that allow these successes to happen. If they are happy with the quality of the product or service your company currently delivers, and they trust you and feel comfortable with your brand, then if you take the trouble to find out what else they might buy from you, and offer it to them at a rate as good as or better than they can get from anywhere else, the odds are that they will buy it.

If you can manage to create a strong corporate brand like Virgin, which is capable of stretching across many product lines, there are likely to be many opportunities to form marketing partnerships. But even if you have a brand that is relatively restricting, by bringing partners' brands into play, there are still ways to sell more to your customers and increase your yield. The better known your brand, and the better known the product you intend to market, the easier your task will be (see Table 8.1).

Table 8.1: The brand/product awareness matrix

Known brand Known product **EASY**	Known brand New product **HARD**
New brand Known product **HARD**	New brand New product **VERY HARD**

By carefully selecting the right partner(s) to work with, and finding the right range of offers to put in front of your customers, you can create a powerful relationship tool. Partnership marketing delivers many benefits, including:

- The giving of more and more tangible value to customers through a wider range of products and services, which reduces expensive churn and increases loyalty to your company and brands.
- The generation of more revenue from the same number of customers, customers that you have already incurred expense in attracting to you.
- The addition of real intangible value to the relationship you already have with your customers. By ensuring your offers are relevant to their needs, represent good value, and are easy to take up, you will be seen as being helpful and not as trying to exploit the relationship.

TYPES OF MARKETING PARTNERSHIPS

Marketing partnerships can take many forms, and the relationship between your two companies can be as simple or as complex as you want to make it. Here are some of the more commonly used methods.

No shared branding

At one extreme, you can agree merely to promote another company to your customers by recommending their products or services. There is no bringing together of brands, and you might earn a revenue per sale or some similar arrangement.

The benefit of this arrangement is that it involves very little work on your part, and you can earn some extra revenue. Importantly, it is an easy arrangement to get out of should you find that things aren't working out the way you might have liked. The downside is that it does little to enhance your own brand, or your relationship with your customer. Indeed, shallow partnerships like this risk causing damage to both your brand and your customer relationship, because typically your partner company isn't working closely enough to your company to echo your culture and core values.

Examples of this type of partnership in action might be where you buy a motor insurance policy, and you take car breakdown cover as an extension to the policy. Typically, the insurer doesn't provide this service and it is sourced from a third-party supplier. It provides you with a chance to buy the cover more cheaply than if you bought it direct from the breakdown company, and the insurer earns a commission on the sale to you.

Let's say you needed to use the breakdown service, but they failed to turn up and help you. There is very little the insurer can do but refer you back to the breakdown company. You would feel upset that they recommended the supplier but appear unwilling to help, and so you would probably go to another insurer when your policy needed to be renewed. The failure on the part of the partner, the breakdown company, has damaged your relationship with the insurer.

The co-branded offering

The next level might be where you add your company's brand alongside that of your chosen partner. Each brand has an equal weighting. Here, your degree of commitment to the marketing partnership has been turned up a notch. You are likely to work jointly on the marketing plan and individual communications. And, because your brand is so prominent, you will need to take much more interest in what your partner is up to in servicing your customer. You might want to think about agreeing standards for levels of service and have reports each month to make sure they are delivered to those standards.

A successful co-branded product might pave the way for a fully branded offering of your own in the future. However, there are certain things you should keep in mind when considering co-branding as a business development initiative, particularly concerning the brand fit.

It is extremely important that you choose partners for co-branding that have similar values to those of your own brand, and who are likely to attract similar target audiences. While the idea of co-branding, apart from sharing marketing costs, is to widen your target audience base and offer more benefits to your own customers, it is no good co-branding with another brand that hits an audience that won't be interested in your products and services. For example, it wouldn't be a good idea for Gucci to co-brand with Coca-Cola—there is no brand character or audience fit. It might be a good idea, though, for Gucci to entertain a co-branding campaign with a champagne or luxury car brand. Similarly, Nike might fit with a golf brand, but not with a retirement planning brand. Great brands are built on consistency, and this applies to co-branding as well.

Using partners to represent your brand

At the other extreme is a proposition where yours is the sole brand attached to the product or service being presented to the customer. What we mean by this is where a partner company supplies goods or services to consumers under your brand name, without using their brand name at all. This type of arrangement requires a major commitment from your company. There is likely to be a large degree of integration of processes and systems with the partner, to ensure that the customer sees a "seamless service." For example, if the partner is running a customer-facing call center on your behalf, they would need to be given access to your customer records within the call center. This means creating new interfaces between your system and the partner's system, or installing your own equipment in the call center, linked to your systems.

One of the main pitfalls to avoid here is misrepresentation of your brand. It is very important that you are convinced the partner is the right one for your brand and will, at all times, represent it in the way you would. Good brand management demands full brand control, whether directly or indirectly, and many companies have found out the hard way that placing their brands in the hands of others can be detrimental to their brand image. So, careful selection is necessary, and training of their staff should be carried out to your satisfaction, so that the brand values you need to be communicated are done so correctly.

Any or all of these partnering approaches may be right for you. You can also see them as a process of natural progression. You might want to start with a simple partnering arrangement, and as your awareness and confidence grows, increase the level of branding and integration.

PARTNERING—THE PROCESS

The process to create your partnership strategy isn't too dissimilar to that for your CRM strategy, as can be seen in Figure 8.1 and the description that follows.

Figure 8.1: The partnering process

What do you have that might be
attractive to potential partners?

↓

Brainstorm what else you might
be able to sell to your customers

↓

Research the demand for further
goods and services,
and your choice of potential partners,
with your existing customers

↓

Develop a partnering strategy
and supporting marketing plan

Step 1: What will attract potential partners?

You need to be able to build a sales proposition to take to a potential marketing partner. Why might they be interested in working with you? Take stock of your assets, and use questions like these as a checklist:

- How many customers do you have in total? How many is this likely to grow to in 12 months' time?
- What data do you hold about them? How old is the data? How complete is it? (This is all information you will already have from your CRM data audit.)
- What recent marketing activity have you undertaken? How responsive were customers to it?
- What distribution channels do you have available to potential partners? How many different means might they have available to market to your customer base?
- What advertising and marketing activities do you have planned that they may be able to "piggyback"?
- What are your core competencies as a company?
- What is your vision?
- What are your core brand values?
- What type of culture exists within the company?

The two companies in Case Study 14 illustrate how CRM can be used as a business-to-business brand-building tool.

Case Study 14
PROVISIONSHOP
Business-to-Business CRM

ProvisionShop is a new consumer brand with an interesting business model. To the end-consumer, ProvisionShop is a generic brand for small retail outlets, but to ProvisionShop's business partners it is a whole lot more. It is delivering a whole set of added-value services to small shopkeepers, which not only constitutes CRM in the business-to-business context, but also enables shopkeepers to deliver CRM to their end-customers. This initiative brings CRM within reach of small businesses, where the cost of employing someone to design, build, and implement a CRM solution would probably be a deterrent.

ProvisionShop will offer its business partners access to the following resources:

- Central ordering and liaison into more than 500 suppliers. This allows ProvisionShop to leverage the total buying requirements of the entire network of outlets and thus maximize its discounts.
- Provision of finance and credit facilities.
- Relevant bespoke operational and expert systems.
- Central business, management, and industry training facilities, through ProvisionShop University.
- Shared staff training costs and access to a pool of ready-trained staff.
- Shared advertising and promotion skills and costs.
- Outlet design, renovation, and set-up—accelerating the speed to market of new outlets.
- Central customer contact center, enabling cost-effective communications to support marketing and relationship-building initiatives.
- "Off-the-shelf" loyalty programs to retain customers, encourage referrals, and maximize yields.

As ProvisionShop's founder and chairman Kenneth Kam says, "In the new century, the consumer relationship industry is evolving in a fast and exciting way. Those companies that develop their capability to become much more intimately involved in a sustainable way with consumers will spearhead the heart of this revolution. Our company is committed to enabling everyday businesses to add intimacy to their customer relationships."

ProvisionShop is an excellent example of a company that has looked at the skills and resources it already has available, and is making those same skills accessible to its business partners. If you take a good look within your organization, you may well see a similar bundle of skills or resources.

NESTLÉ

Nestlé posed a similar question to us a couple of years ago in one country. The problem they put before us was, how could they make Nestlé the first-choice brand for small coffee-shop operators? The advertising agency was looking at all sorts of brand promotion, while we came at it from another angle. The questions in our mind were: How can Nestlé make a difference to the daily running of these businesses? And how can Nestlé give something to these businesses that they can't afford to lose?

We looked beyond the products themselves and at Nestlé as an organization. What skills and resources did it have that might be useful to the shop operators? We came up with a list of services:

- **Legal services team**: These could be made available to help with lease negotiations and resolution of disputes.
- **Purchasing power**: Nestlé's buyers could negotiate on behalf of the distribution network to obtain discounts on supplying hobs, water boilers, signage, tables and chairs, and any other items of significant expenditure. These savings would go straight to the operator's bottom line.
- **Marketing and promotional skills**: Nestlé could offer assistance in creating an awareness of the coffee shop and in designing/running promotions.
- **Finances**: The company could provide access to Nestlé's financial team, to assist with putting together sensible business plans, managing the accounts, auditing, and so on. For many of these small businesses, business finance is a necessary evil. Being led through it by the skills of a major organization such as Nestlé would be invaluable.

In some markets, core products and services can be easily replicated, making it difficult to differentiate your offer from that of a competitor. Taking an alternate view, as demonstrated through the ProvisionShop and Nestlé examples, could allow you to forge deeper relationships with your customers that go beyond price or product. Once they become used to receiving this assistance and guidance from you, it will be incredibly difficult for them to move to another supplier. So, the question is: What can you offer your business partners?

Step 2: What else might you be able to sell to your customers?

You need to refer back to the data collected about your customers' lifestyles. What are they doing day in, day out? What do they need to buy that you could reasonably sell to them? Start off by looking for things that have a simple association with your core business and where it is easy for the customer to see why you are offering it to them. If it is too removed from your core business, you are unlikely to be successful.

For example, a colleague working at Norwich Union created a marketing partnership with one of the U.K.'s largest mobile phone networks and offered a free mobile phone to customers. This was marketed on the back of Norwich Union's Club Motor Insurance policy. It was positioned as the means to contact the 24-hour emergency rescue center wherever you might be. The point was made that having a 24-hour rescue service for accidents and breakdowns was fine, but how would you contact the service? This was a natural extension of the basic service.

However, if Norwich Union had written to customers offering to supply new television sets, it might have been difficult for the customer to understand why the company they bought insurance from had suddenly become a retailer of TV sets. In fact, it would be possible for Norwich Union to supply TV sets to the customers' door at highly competitive prices, because of the number of sets they bought each year to fulfill claims on home insurance policies. But the point is, the customer would never have been able to make the connection, and that is key. Always make your CRM offerings relevant to the consumer and your brand proposition.

Step 3: Research your ideas

Test out your extra product ideas within focus groups. You may feel you understand what you can sell to your customers, but you are about to venture into new waters, and the more information you can obtain, the better prepared you will be. Check that the product offers make sense, that they are competitive in your customers' view, that your candidate partners are companies they feel comfortable with, and that your marketing concept makes sense and gets your desired message across. Going through this process will be time and money well spent. CRM is about dialogue and listening to customers.

Step 4: Selecting potential partners

The selection of a marketing partner is a responsibility that should not be taken lightly. An amazing number of such deals are put together under informal circumstances, such as on the golf course; a bit of discussion on the first tee and the whole thing is sealed by the second green. But we are talking about two companies working together for an extended period of time, and there is no point in going into such an arrangement thinking of it as something to do for a few months and see how it goes. This is a strategic undertaking, and the selection of a partner requires a rigorous process, almost as if you were acquiring the company—it is not "due diligence," of course, but it is pretty close.

In CRM partnerships you have to bring two companies together at a number of levels. It is not enough that they each have a product that their customers might want. There are a number of other things to consider in finding your ideal partner:

- **Brand and market position**
  - ○ Do your brands sit comfortably together, if you are looking to co-brand? Are the brand values similar?
  - ○ Is there mutual respect and trust between your organizations?
- **Corporate culture**
  - ○ How well matched are your corporate cultures?
  - ○ Can your people work together?
  - ○ Do they want to?
- **Partnering objectives**
  - ○ Do your companies share a similar vision for the partnering activity?

- ○ Do you both see it as a long-term arrangement? A win–win situation?
- ○ Are you both willing to see it through to the end, despite possible problems?
- **Information**
  - ○ What information needs to be shared?
  - ○ How easy will it be to move information between your systems?
  - ○ How willing are you to share information with each other?
- **Commercial arrangements**
  - ○ Can you agree the basis of the contractual and financial arrangements between your companies?
  - ○ Will it be worthwhile for both partners and their respective customer bases?
- **Resourcing the work**
  - ○ What resources—people, systems, distribution channels, products—does your prospective partner have available? Can they fulfill in practice what they are offering to you?
- **Previous partnering experience**
  - ○ Can they show you examples of previous joint marketing work they have undertaken? How successful were they?

While the main attraction will be the new revenue stream that partnering represents to your company, go into it with your eyes wide open. Remember, the reason that you have the opportunity to begin with is that you have excelled in the service you have provided to your customers up until now. Because of this, your customers will allow you to offer them new good products and services. But be careful, because if you or your marketing partner fail in the delivery of the new product or service, that failure could cause permanent damage to your brand image, and therefore to your core business. It is important that you protect your brand at all times.

Make sure that you retain ultimate responsibility for contact with your customers. Ensure that you know what is going on at all times by continually monitoring the performance of your team and your partner's team. Think of it as you would a parental role. You want to see your new infant learn and develop, but at the same time you want to ensure that nothing valuable gets damaged in the process.

Step 5: Defining your marketing programs

Once you have selected your partner(s), you need to work closely with them to develop your tactical marketing programs. In this newly formed marriage, there must be give and take. Customers that you think are good prospects may not be as attractive to your partner, and vice versa. You need to find groups of people who you both agree are worth marketing to. You will have to be led to a degree by your partner, as that partner will be led by you, because, after all, it is their core business and you are likely to have selected them because they are one of the best in their field. However, you will be likely to know the best way to get your own customers to respond to approaches. So, the key is to use each other's skills to your mutual benefit.

In particular, you need to agree who you are going to sell to, which brand you will be using, the offer you are going to put to the customer, how you are going to communicate it, and how you will fulfill the offer when they respond.

Define each other's roles and responsibilities for the entire process

This is an area that, for some reason, often tends to be overlooked in partnering. There are frequently covert assumptions made about who is going to do what, when sensibly this should be talked about and agreed up-front. This may sound like common sense, but it is easy to get it wrong. You need to sketch out the whole sales and marketing to fulfillment process, and agree who is to do what and by when. For the fulfillment process especially, you need to clearly define proposed service levels to ensure that customers are not kept waiting for their goods.

Share feedback

Share information on responses with your partner. If they are not as good as you had hoped for, work with your partner to gradually refine and improve the way you work together. Like a marriage, you cannot expect everything to be perfect from the outset, but if you recognize each other's strengths, communicate effectively, and trust and respect each other, you will build a strong partnership and reap the rewards.

MAINTAINING YOUR CRM PROGRAM

It is all too easy to breathe a great sigh of relief the moment your program launches into the market, and then sit back expecting or hoping for the best. Unfortunately, the reality is that this is where much of your work begins. Once you are in the public domain, everyone will start to analyze your creation—your customers, your competitors, the media, your board, management, and employees.

Once your program is "live," you have to make it deliver. You have to ensure that your customers receive everything you promise them and more, and you need to make sure that your program is meeting your financial plan, and adjust it if necessary. You are in the spotlight—if it goes well, there will be a line of people trying to take the credit; but if it goes wrong, you will suddenly find yourself alone.

To help avoid problems and failure, ensure that you are getting all the management information you need in order to know exactly what is happening within your program at all times. Management information is often a part of the program that evolves, as it may be difficult to envisage what information you need until the program starts to run. So, ensure that you have at least a minimum amount of information available at the outset; then, once you have a better idea of your needs, ask your systems team to build them for you. Having up-to-date information will help you to monitor and adjust your program as it develops.

STAYING AHEAD OF THE PACK—KEEPING THE COMPETITION GUESSING

Once word of your program gets out, you can be certain that your competitors will analyze what you have done. How they respond will depend on how big a threat they perceive you to be. The likelihood is that they will develop their own variant of your program if they see any merit in what you have achieved, and they will retaliate when they see the impact you are having on their share of the market.

We always advocate a strategy that means you don't reveal all your hand in one go. Plan your implementation in such a way that you implement new features to your program every four to six months in the early days. In this way, even if your competitors try to copy what you have done, by the time they launch their version, you will be ready to launch your next part. For example, when Tesco launched their Clubcard loyalty program, by the time their main competitor (Sainsbury) had responded with their own Reward program, Tesco were ready to launch their Clubcard Plus, which included a personal banking account and store credit facility within the card.

Even without trying to confuse the competition, there are reasons to keep your program developing. You need to keep it interesting for your customers. If they feel a program is stagnating or dying, they are likely to quickly lose interest in it and drop away. Part of your CRM implementation should therefore be to look at the post-launch phase, and plan what you want to launch and when. Then you need to ensure that you have the resources in place to continue to develop the program beyond its launch state. This is, unfortunately, another area where many projects fail to make adequate provision. Often, once the program is launched, the project team is broken up and sent back to their original jobs. CRM shouldn't be viewed as a project. You are changing the way your organization behaves forever, and you need to have a management system and team in place within the organization to oversee the program for the long term.

TRACKING THE IMPACT OF YOUR CRM PROGRAM

The CRM program you have implemented, or want to implement, should reflect the brand values of your company. One way to judge the effectiveness of CRM is therefore to track your brand values against the competition. You can limit the tracking to values reflected by the CRM program itself, by specifically limiting research to questions related to the program and the brand values. Alternatively, you could have a section in the overall corporate brand tracking research specifically on the CRM initiative. Whichever approach you choose, it is very important that the brand values performance of the company is tracked against the competition to see where gains are being realized and where more effort needs to be put in. The really smart companies also track their brand values against the best brands in other industries— companies they don't compete with—so that they can benchmark themselves against the brands that have very high esteem in the minds of consumers.

Many countries have developed tools to measure brand performance. Whatever method you use, it is important to get an assessment of how your brand is doing.

If you are also tracking the financial value of your brand, as well as the customer equity aspects, then monitoring the influence of the CRM program will be important, as any CRM program is likely to be a key driver of brand value. Indeed, the weighting of this particular driver will probably increase over time if the program is doing well. The best brand valuation model we have come across is that created by Brand Finance plc (www.brandfinance.com).

Your CRM program will undoubtedly enhance the value and equity of your brand. It will build customer relationships, increase brand loyalty, attract new customers, and make your brand a true friend to all of your customers. Through dialogue and interaction, CRM will make your customers feel appreciated and wanted. They will feel genuine affection for your brand. A well-planned and executed CRM program will put the romance back into your brand–customer relationship.

9

New Media: The Challenges for Branding and CRM

Many companies that have returned to the "Mom and Pop store" mentality in their customer relationships in recent years have found themselves facing a new challenge with the advent of the Internet and other new media.

The World Wide Web, mobile communication, and digital television provide us with a mass of opportunities to get closer to our customers whilst, paradoxically, in many ways becoming more remote. These technologies provide a means by which we can recognize the individual customer we are communicating with, and allow us to tailor the style of the communication to the specifications of each customer. For example, many websites allow people to customize the way the site appears when they enter it. Even if they don't register with the site and reveal who they are, by using techniques such as "cookies," companies can recognize them and welcome them back when they return. For some people, this can lead to the feeling that "Big Brother" is watching them, and for all but the full-blown "Web-head" this can be very unnerving.

INTERNET TRADING AND ISSUES OF TRUST

It is interesting that trading on the Internet generates more nervousness among consumers than does trading over the telephone or purchasing goods via the TV set. It has been observed that when we are watching television, we tend to sit back in our seat. This is a non-confrontational posture. However, when we use a PC, we tend to lean forward, which is an aggressive posture. Perhaps there is something in this—or it may be just that we are used to having a TV set in the house. For years, we have relied on it for news and information, so we have come to trust it. Whatever the reason for the discrepancy, we believe that, in marketing terms, the Web will only really take off when it and the TV set merge. In the U.S. and the U.K., we are already starting to see TV sets with built-in modems.

The U.K. has 22 million households and around 60 million people. Currently in the U.K., around one in three adults regularly use the Internet, either at home or in the office. Almost every home has a TV set. The convergence of the Net and the TV will make the Web accessible to the masses, and that is what will drive volume trading on to the Net. Less than one in 10 people in the U.K. have ever bought anything over the Net. Of those that have, typically it has been small-ticket items such as books or CDs from Amazon.com or a similar company. People are buying low-cost items from well-known brands.

It is all about trust. There still is a complete lack of confidence in the Web and the companies who trade on it. Just look at the way technology stocks plummeted in value during 2000 and early 2001. The general opinion of the financial press is that many of the early Internet marketing companies were in it for a fast buck and are no longer around to tell the tale. In 2000, a number of very high profile Internet companies called in the receivers. This has made it very difficult for dotcom companies to obtain funding within the market, as investors remain nervous. This is not surprising when companies like lastminute.com were floated without having ever made any profit, and at a value many times the price they would have been valued at in a traditional business investment scenario. Investors saw their share value just slip away. In the 21st century, venture capitalists are much more cautious, and a new sense of realism has set in. When stories of major Web brands failures are constantly hitting the headlines, it is understandable that consumers are going to be wary of dealing with them.

Aligned to this, some major organizations, such as Microsoft, Barclays Bank, and America Online, have been in the headlines because their database security has been breached. Is it any wonder that people are unsure as to whether they can trust an online company to look after their personal information? As we have said, being able to trust the brand is fundamental to being able to build a long-term relationship with your customer.

GETTING YOURSELF ON TO THE WEB

So, how do you go about preparing your company to trade over the Web? How do you create an atmosphere of trust? And, most of all, how can you build a personal relationship with your customer when the face of your brand becomes a PC or TV screen? You will find the answers to these questions and many more in our book *Hi-Tech Hi-Touch Branding* (John Wiley & Sons, 2001), but one of the key issues for traditional brand companies is the need to keep the Internet brand consistent with the traditional brand offering. Here are two cases of companies (Carphone and Ford) that have recently tried to bring their Web offering more into line with their brand offering, and one completely new Internet start-up company (its4me) that has done things right and embraced CRM from the very beginning.

Case Study 15

CARPHONE WAREHOUSE
Extending the brand experience via the Web

The Carphone Warehouse is the U.K.'s largest independent mobile phone retailer. According to its advertising, it offers "impartial advice" on the combination of phone, network, and tariff that best fits a customer's needs.

The Carphone Warehouse has moved into CRM by building a new website which bundles up its expertise and delivers it to the customer at the customer's own convenience. It provides answers to all the likely questions a customer will ask and then guides them toward the best fit of phone and network.

Lesley Angus, group marketing director at The Carphone Warehouse, explained the company's reasons for building the website: "We felt that a website was a natural extension of our existing retail and direct brand experience. It would be a further method to communicate, provide advice, and offer services to customers. With the market growth, many customers would also require us to provide a website. The Internet has additional appeal to us due to its convergence with the mobile communication products we specialize in selling. The Internet as a medium allows us to enhance the product and services we offer. Finally, we also recognized the fit between our technology-aware customer base and Internet users."

At the same time as delivering a functionally rich site for the customer, The Carphone Warehouse was keen to reflect its brand values with the site. "We wanted something completely distinct from our competitors and something highly interactive," said Angus. "It had to position The Carphone Warehouse as the communications authority and be a center for impartial information on the industry. It was also essential that it was built on a platform that would allow us to build and sustain a meaningful relationship with our customers."

The site is supported by a system and database that contains details of the various mobile phones, airtime providers, and pricing structures available. The site asks customers to enter information about themselves, their lifestyle, and the amount of use they expect to make of a mobile phone. The site then gives an accurate recommendation of the deal that suits them best.

By the end of the first three weeks of trading, the site was performing at the level of a new store opening, with most payments handled online. The Carphone Warehouse is optimistic that their business will continue to grow. Angus explained: "This is a highly efficient way of targeting potentially millions of customers, without the overheads of our other sales channels."

Case Study 16
FORD U.K.
Creating a seamless brand experience

In November 2000, Ford U.K. launched its new consumer-driven website www.ford.co.uk. In doing so, it created a seamless brand experience for consumers by bringing together all of its Web properties, including the newly launched Ford Journey online sales channel, Ford Credit, and the Ford Customer Service Division.

The new site includes intelligence that allows tailoring of the site and its content based on each customer's interests and previous Web surfing behavior. The site has been designed to emphasize Ford's focus on building relationships with its customers over time. Ford ensures that a link to its privacy policy is visible at all times. This explains to the customer how Ford will protect any information given by the customer.

"We are delighted with the insight which consumers have given us on the look and feel of this new site. The soft images are such a contrast to the technologically advanced framework that drives them. This first stage creates the foundation for an even higher specification site, and further enhancements will be complete in the next few months," said Graham Whickman, CRM manager, Ford of Britain. This Web solution has been developed as a pan-European platform and will be rolled out across all Ford's European operations during 2001.

So, major high street brands are beginning to see the importance of aligning their websites with what they offer through their stores and forecourts. This means keeping the brand imagery consistent, and conveying the essence of the brand proposition through the features and functions delivered to the customer via the site.

Existing brands hooking up to the Web have the benefit of having gained the trust of consumers over a number of years. But what if you are looking to launch a completely new brand, and a brand that is looking to major in sales over the Web? Let's take a look at a new U.K. company that has done just that.

Case Study 17
its4me PLC
Hi-tech Hi-touch branding on the Internet

Introduction

In late 1999, two senior figures from the U.K. insurance industry, Patrick Smith and Paul Cheall, got together to launch a new company and a new brand into the marketplace. Their ambition was to launch an online insurance intermediary to sell motor, home, and other general insurance products over the Internet.

Smith has a strong track record in building financial services companies, having launched in the U.K. private health insurance companies, and direct motor and home insurers, and developed high street insurance brokerages. He has a habit of challenging the conventional thinking of the marketplace while never losing sight of the bottom line. Smith saw the opportunity the Internet provided to revolutionize the insurance sector by stripping out the costs from the traditional distribution process, while at the same time seizing the opportunity to tailor the product and the service as closely as possible to the needs of individual customers. The opportunity was to offer better value in terms of products and service directly to the customer, while reducing costs for the company and the customer.

The brand name

The brand name created was "its4me." "The thinking behind this was to take a basic product and give consumers the maximum opportunity to personalize it," Smith explained. "its4me conveys one of the most important aspects of our business philosophy—personal attention and personalized products. We agree it's not the normal type of insurance company name, and it reflects our innovative approach to business. We are new and we are different, and we aim to break the mould."

So, how was the company created, and how did it aim to gain credibility in the eyes of consumers? The launch project began in February 2000, having secured venture capital backing from a major international financial services company. its4me is fully funded for at least the first five years of operation, which puts it in a strong position to be able to build the business without concerns about finding more funding. Many major Internet brands have struggled to secure second-round funding, especially in 2000.

The business model

The starting point for the its4me plc business model is the creation of a panel of insurance companies who can supply motor and home insurance products electronically to its4me. The products are offered for sale on the its4me.co.uk website. Consumers enter their details and obtain a quotation instantly online, pay for it online, and view and print their policy documentation online. The system will then send an electronic data interchange (EDI) message to the relevant insurer, giving details of the policy that has been sold. In the event that the customer wants to change their policy, they simply log on to the system and make the changes themselves.

There is no need for any human intervention from the first point of contact to conclusion—there is just the system and the customer. This results in minimal cost and maximum efficiency. Where insurance is sold through a traditional insurance intermediary, there is a lot of delay and duplication. This all means cost, the potential for errors, and a slow service for the customer. And the best part is that, being Internet-based, the system is available 24/7, 365 days a year. Try finding a regular broker in the physical world who will sell you a policy at 2 a.m.!

So, that is its4me's recipe for happy insurance customers. Or is it? Well, not really. You see, a big part of the model is missing, and that is the reality check. There are people who want the clinical efficiency of a system, but there are just as many, if not more, who want the warmth of a relationship. its4me recognized this from the outset and believes that what it has put together will set it apart from other emerging e-insurance companies.

Let's go back a bit. In 2000, only about one-third of the U.K.'s 60 million population were regularly accessing the Internet, either at home, work, or college, and probably no more than 10% were regularly buying goods and services over the Web. This meant that the vast majority of people still weren't using the Web; in particular, they still weren't buying over the Net. In insurance terms, according to Fletcher Research, only around 400,000 of the U.K.'s 25 million or so vehicles would be insured over the Web in 2000.

It seemed that people were using the Web as a source of information, but when it came to the point of purchase, they used more traditional methods. Why? Trust. People trust brands. But its4me was a new brand. Back to the same question: how could it gain the consumer's trust? It is one thing getting brand awareness, but it is another matter entirely to get consumer trust. Lastminute.com, in the U.K., actually reached an 84% brand awareness level but only a 17% trust figure.

In finalizing its business model, its4me realized that:

- For the foreseeable future, the majority of the insurance business was offline, moving online.
- It needed to establish itself as providing not only great products, but also great service.
- The key to gaining the trust of the customer was by making itself available to the customer in as many different ways as possible. It needed to create a human face to the company, which allowed customers to build a relationship with the brand.

So, when the final model was put together, it looked something like this:

- The customer, if he or she so wishes, has the ability to buy customized insurance on a fully self-service basis. They enter their personal details, the system calculates the relevant premium, they pay online by credit or debit card, or they set up a direct debit online. Once the payment is accepted, they can browse their policy documentation online and print it on their own printer in the comfort of their home. There is no need to talk to anyone, so there is no pressure selling. They simply get what they need delivered efficiently.

- However, at any point in the process, if assistance is required, its4me has, waiting in the wings, a team of insurance professionals ready to help. The means of contacting them is up to the personal preference of the individual customer:

  o The system includes a searchable help facility and glossary of insurance terms, which works in a similar way to what you might find within the Microsoft Office products.

  o The customer can click on an icon to send an email to the team with a query. its4me publishes a service level on its site saying that all emails will be responded to within one hour, and it consistently beats that target by a significant margin.

  o Customers can open up an interactive text chat session. This is a very direct means of having real time dialogue with the team across the Internet. This facility allows questions to be answered immediately. its4me's staff can help the customer complete the on-screen forms remotely via a collaborative viewing facility, and they can even "push" help pages through to the customer's screen using the software. They can also "push" through an image of the team member the customer is having an online dialogue with. This helps to personalize the service even more.

○ The customer can elect to ring the team, or request the
   team to call them back at an allotted time.

its4me is also able to complete the entire process for the
customer over the phone if they so wish.

Customer intimacy and empowerment

Empowering the customer to customize the product, and the
way the service is delivered to them, has given its4me a real
means of differentiating itself, as well as the ability to gain
customer confidence in a marketplace where customers are
still more than a little nervous of e-commerce companies and
still believe that the Internet means low cost but zero service.
It recognizes that other companies will be able to obtain
similar products from their insurers, that other companies can
probably build a similar processing system, but that what will
make a difference over the long term is service quality—and
that means people.

The Internet doesn't have to mean remoteness of contact.
There are many ways to build a bond with customers if you
just think differently. As we write this case study, its4me is in
the process of installing a webcam in its offices so that
customers can see the team at work—ready to leap to their
assistance. Its4me is a great example of hi-tech hi-touch
branding using CRM techniques. You can visit the site at
its4me.co.uk.

USEFUL CRM INTERNET BRANDING TIPS

The Web has the ability to become an immensely powerful medium for
the customer to get what they need very quickly and from a massive
choice of providers, not just in their own country, but potentially
anywhere in the world.

The Web gives us, as marketers, the mechanism to learn more about
our customers and their buying behavior than any other development

since Mom and Pop stores came into being. All that is needed is for the links to the Web to become faster and more reliable, for the Web to be integrated into objects that we inherently trust, such as the TV set, and for us to really understand how to market effectively via the Web.

Using the Web effectively doesn't mean cramming as many links and flashing banners on to a page as possible in the hope of tempting the visitor. What makes a website appealing and effective is, to a degree, subjective, but here are a few guidelines to get you started:

- **Make your site useful to your visitor**: Your site should be "fit for the purpose," in the same way that your physical product is. It must "do what it says on the can"—that is, it must deliver exactly what your visitor expects. If your site is there to give out information, the visitor must be able to find what they need quickly and easily. If you are selling online, make it easy for the customer to see how to buy.
- **Make your site intuitive**: Design your site in such a way that the user can immediately see what to do next. Use buttons with descriptions that tell the customer what will happen if they click—words like "next" don't do that; in fact, they can increase the user's anxiety about transacting on the Web. Try not to rely on the user visiting your help screens, because often they just won't bother. Watch friends and family, or focus groups, to see how people who are unfamiliar with the site find their way around it.
- **Keep the site as simple as possible**: Try not to overload the site with a mass of graphics and animations. The site may run quickly through your dedicated link, but for the average user dialing in over a phone line, it just means waiting time while the graphics load. Keep the site simple, clean, and easy to navigate, and you will make more sales.
- **Plan to regularly update your site, particularly the home page**: If you want people to keep coming back to your site, you must update the content regularly, otherwise pretty soon they will be visiting your competitors.
- **Above all, make the site interesting and entertaining**: You want your visitors to feel that they have gained something by spending time at your site, so much so that they will add your site to their "favorites" or "bookmarks" and tell all their friends about it.

The principles of designing your website are similar to CRM: you have to make it easy for the customer to do business with you; keep the process as simple as possible; make sure that you are adding value to that person's life through their visit to your site; and, above all, design by thinking from the customer inward. Ask yourself what they want from your site. The answer will tell you what the site needs to do and what it should look like. For a comprehensive look at website branding and CRM, we suggest you read our book *Hi-Tech Hi-Touch Branding*.

The following case study provides a final example of good CRM practice on the Internet.

Case Study 18
SONY (AUSTRALIA)
Launching a new product on the Internet

December 2000 saw the launch, in Australia, of PlayStation.com. Developed by Sony in conjunction with SAP and PricewaterhouseCoopers, PlayStation.com is a fully integrated e-tailing solution. It allows customers to browse through products in an online store, adding merchandise to their virtual shopping carts as they go. When they have finished shopping, the system allows them to pay for their goods online using their credit card via a secure server link.

PlayStation.com's screen system is linked into a "back office" administration system that allows Sony to manage the entire customer contact cycle. This integration is critical to ensure high satisfaction levels throughout the customer's entire contact cycle with Sony—from the ordering, to the delivery, to the ongoing support. It also means that Sony Computer Entertainment Australia and PlayStation.com can improve their cost-effectiveness and profitability through streamlined management and reporting procedures, said Chris Bennett, managing director and CEO, SAP Australia and New Zealand.

The overall design of the PlayStation.com solution will allow the company to continue to add features and functionality according to customer needs, thereby delivering the "sticky" characteristics that an e-tailing site requires today.

Michael Ephraim, managing director, Sony Computer Entertainment Australia, said "We feel PlayStation.com will further build the brand equity that PlayStation™ has established over the years and deliver the same level of excitement and entertainment that PlayStation™, PS One™, and PlayStation™ 2 have offered to the over 1.7 million purchasers so far in Australia of our products."

Huge demand is predicted for the Australian launch of PlayStation.com based on the response to the global launch in Japan in March 2000 that saw 600,000 hits against the website in the first two minutes of operation. A total of 980,000 orders were placed in the first week of the global launch, with approximately 33% of these being placed on the website.

In preparation for the PlayStation 2 launch, PlayStation.com has set up a call center. The system allows the call center operators to have a single view of PlayStation.com customers. Operators have visibility of customer orders, and can help customers with order status enquiries, placement of orders, changes to orders, and questions regarding availability of stock. This accessibility to accurate, real-time information will help them to deliver exceptional service to customers.

The data that Sony can collect through PlayStation.com holds massive potential:

• Sony already has 1.7 million PlayStation™ customers in Australia—that is, 1.7 million people who will need to buy games and peripherals for the PlayStation™ and PlayStation™ 2.

  Most of the profit on console systems comes from after-sales—that is, games. By creating a PlayStation™ 2 e-newsletter and mailing it regularly to these customers, offering deals in conjunction with the games manufacturers, Sony could drive up revenues. The newsletter could also promote up-and-coming releases and generate demand in advance.

Whenever a new console is launched, a bunch of dedicated magazines spring up on the shelves, for which customers pay a lot of money each month, so there is no doubting the demand. It would reinforce the brand and keep customers coming back to the site to find details of the games being promoted in the newsletter.

- The next stage would be to have each customer register on the Playstation.com site so that they login each time. This way, Sony can track its most active customers and potentially focus their activities. It would also mean that Sony could begin to learn what type of games or peripherals each customer was showing interest in. This data could be used each time a new game was released to use direct email notifications to those customers most likely to buy based on previous ordering or interest areas.

- As the database grows and the communications develop, Sony will have a ready-made communication device to take orders for PS3!

Source: SAP and Sony

10

Romancing Your Customer: Are You Ready?

We hope that you have found this book enjoyable. Our aim is not only to discuss the technical aspects of branding and CRM, but also to demonstrate how they can be applied in the real world and to illustrate the challenges you are likely to face. We have alerted you to the likely sources of these challenges, so that you can prepare for them in advance.

In this final chapter, we summarize the key learning points from each chapter.

Chapter 1: CRM and Brand Value

- CRM represents a fantastic opportunity for anyone wishing to build a corporate brand, because it assists in the rapid buildup of both brand equity and brand value.
- CRM creates differentiation. This helps to grow market share and, thus, to build the financial value of the brand.
- CRM helps to build brands *quickly*. It accelerates both the learning curve about the customer and the development of the brand–customer relationship. It is the future of brand building.

Chapter 2: CRM Explained

- CRM is all about collaborating with your customer. It is concerned with creating the classic win–win situation, where you add value to your customer's daily life, and they give you loyalty in return.

- Not all customers are equal. The Pareto principle (80:20 rule), which holds that approximately 80% of your profits come from 20% of your customers, applies to nearly every business situation.
- The purpose of a CRM program is to recognize your best customers and hold on to them. It also has the aim of transforming lower-value customers into higher-value ones.
- Effective CRM is about applying the knowledge you have about your customer every time they interact with you, in such a way that you add value to your product or service, and thus strengthen the emotional bond between the customer, your brand, and your company.
- CRM is not a fantastic new technique that has been created for the 21st century. It was being practiced back in the days when Mom and Pop stores predominated in retailing.
- Many CRM programs take the form of points-based loyalty schemes; however, generally speaking, points-based schemes do little to improve the loyalty of customers.
- CRM is not something that can give impact to your business overnight. The real payback will come over time, but it will be real, and it will be permanent.
- We have yet to come across a single organization or business that would not derive real benefits from CRM.
- CRM allows you do the unthinkable—to benefit your customer and yourself at the same time.

Chapter 3: Brand-building Benefits of CRM

- CRM works by:
  - Creating a continuous communication loop between your organization and your customer.
  - Getting to know the customer.
  - Using existing customer data.
  - Asking the customer what they want from you.
  - Establishing customers' unlocked potential.
  - Creating knowledge.
  - Reusing knowledge time after time.

- The benefits of having CRM in your company include:
  - Helping you to build your brand image.
  - Attracting new customers.
  - Selling more to your current customers.
  - Shielding your customers from approaches by your competitors.
  - Increased returns on brand investment.
  - Stronger and cheaper customer acquisition rates.
  - Increased customer referrals.
  - Lower rates of brand defection.
  - Expressing brand personality.
  - Increasing staff loyalty.
  - More effective use of advertising and promotion budgets.
  - Better understanding of the business cost drivers.
  - More effective, relevant product design.
  - Reduced research needs.
  - Increased profits and brand value.
  - Adding value to investor relations.
- Companies that focus on developing a strong relationship with their customers will obtain twice the sales growth of those that do not.
- Those same companies can expect to receive six times the return on equity of those that don't build a bond with their customers.
- The main reason that customers leave is that companies don't talk to them, so they feel unwanted or badly treated.
- Adding value to your brand really means that it has to do one or all of the following:
  - Save customers money.
  - Save them time (time equals money).
  - Save them hassle (offers a quicker/more efficient service).
  - Customize products or services specifically to customer needs.

Chapter 4: Organizing for Brand Management and CRM

- The key question for every manager every day is: *What are you doing today to add value to your customers' lives?*
- In the new-style company, it is not the brand or product manager who is most important—it is the "customer manager."

- Segmentation has always been a key element of any marketing strategy and is vital to the branding process. The better defined the target, the more effective your brand strategy is likely to be.
- Installing your CRM program is a great chance to "spring clean" your processes. Remove those tasks that are being performed each day that add no real value to your customers or your organization.
- Set up a pilot program and monitor its impact.
- Prepare in advance for roadblocks to your CRM project.
- Work through your financial justification for your project as soon as possible.
- Don't neglect your internal marketing.
- Reuse current initiatives wherever possible.
- Find a project champion.
- Make sensible use of outsourcing to speed up your project.
- Plan your migration strategy while your pilot is running.
- The three golden rules before starting your CRM program are:
  ○ Develop clear objectives.
  ○ Make things easy for the customer.
  ○ Be realistic about what you can achieve.

Chapter 5: Building Brand Value through Customer Profitability

- You must establish the profitability of your customers.
- How does the Pareto principle apply to your customer base? Is it 80:20 or 90:10?
- Your money should be seeking out customers who:
  ○ Buy from you regularly.
  ○ Have bought from you recently.
  ○ Are making a significant contribution to your company profits.
  ○ Are recommending your product or service to friends and colleagues.
  ○ Have significant development potential.
- You need to build a profile of your most profitable customers: who they are; where they live; what they do for a living; their family background; their lifestyle.

- Your next priority is to look at the second most profitable group. Who is in this group, and who among them fits the profile of your most profitable customers? What are they doing differently that makes them less profitable for you? How can you use your marketing skills via CRM to change their habits?
- Plug your information gaps by talking to your customer by any means available to you.
- The hub of any CRM initiative must be your marketing database. Without it, you cannot hope to harness the information you have about your customers.
- Look at the recency, frequency, and value of your interactions with your customers and use this to prioritize your CRM activities.
- When you build your CRM program, include tiers to create recognition and to motivate customers within the program to perform in such a way that they reach the next level of value to your company.

Chapter 6: Implementation Strategy

- There are six steps to CRM heaven, and we described how you should proceed with these. They are:
  - Step 1: Auditing your systems.
  - Step 2: Auditing your data.
  - Step 3: Auditing your existing customer relationships.
  - Step 4: Auditing your financials.
  - Step 5: Creating your CRM strategy in line with your brand.
  - Step 6: Creating your tactical CRM initiatives.
- Consider using an agency to help you put your cost case together. Outside help can often overcome problems of internal politics.

Chapter 7: Making Your Brand More Customer-focused

- Here we provided you with a worked example of how to create the financial model for your CRM project.
- Also in this chapter was a complete CRM case history from the motor industry.

Chapter 8: Final Steps and Touches

- Partnership marketing can be seen as a corollary of CRM.
- There is good money to be earned by selling more goods and services to existing customers.
- Partnership marketing is two or more companies working together to market goods or services, create competitive advantage, and generate incremental revenues.
- Creating a high degree of trust in your brand and organization is key to securing the loyalty of your customers over the long term.
- If you have a high degree of brand awareness, and the product you intend to market is well known, your task of securing good partners will be easier.
- By carefully selecting the right partner(s) to work with, and finding the right range of offers to put in front of your customers, you can create a powerful relationship tool.
- The partnering steps:
  - Ask yourself what you have that is attractive to potential partners.
  - Ask yourself what else you might be able to sell to your customers through your partners.
  - Research your ideas.
  - Select your potential partners with care, because your brand image is at stake when you carry out co-branding campaigns.
  - Ensure that there is a good brand fit, in terms of both target audience and brand values.
  - Define your marketing programs carefully, so that each partner is very clear about what is expected of them.
- Once your program is live, you have to make it deliver. You have to ensure that your customers receive everything you promise them—and more. Your brand image depends on it.

Chapter 9: New Media: The Challenges for Branding and CRM

- The Web and other new technologies provide a means by which we can recognize the individual customer we are communicating with, and tailor the style of the communication to the specifications of each customer.

- However, customers are nervous about trading over the Web, unlike trading over the telephone or the TV.
- Being able to trust the brand and the communication medium is fundamental to being able to build a long-term relationship with your customers.
- Whether you are an Internet-based company or one that is trying to establish a presence on the Web, remember that your website is your brand and should reflect everything you want your brand to project. For detailed guidelines on how to build a great website and incorporate CRM techniques, refer to our book *Hi-tech Hi-touch Branding*.

Index